AN INTRODUCTION TO
THE HISTORY OF THE SOCIAL
SCIENCES IN SCHOOLS

AMERICAN

HISTORICAL ASSOCIATION

INVESTIGATION OF THE
SOCIAL STUDIES IN THE SCHOOLS

• •
•

COMMISSION ON DIRECTION

REPORT OF THE COMMISSION
ON THE SOCIAL STUDIES
PART II

AN INTRODUCTION TO THE HISTORY OF THE SOCIAL SCIENCES IN SCHOOLS

BY

HENRY JOHNSON

Professor of History, Teachers College, Columbia University

CHARLES SCRIBNER'S SONS

NEW YORK   CHICAGO   BOSTON   ATLANTA
SAN FRANCISCO   DALLAS

14137

PREFACE

This volume, the second of the series of reports of the Commission on the Social Studies in the Schools, presents Professor Johnson's brief summary of the history of the teaching of the social sciences in the schools. A systematic, detailed history of society's experience with this problem does not exist. The qualifications necessary for the completion of such a task have rarely occurred in any single individual. Only a person familiar with the teaching problems in elementary and secondary education, with the whole field of history, and with a knowledge of the leading languages of Europe could embark upon such a task. The Commission feels itself fortunate in securing Professor Henry Johnson to undertake this work. The deliberations of the Commission have been much enriched by the frequent references to past experience which his life-long study supplied. It was with the desire to give permanence to these contributions and to share with the whole teaching profession the fruits of this labor that the Commission authorized Professor Johnson to prepare this volume.

Circumstances would not permit the completion of the more comprehensive and detailed history of the teaching of these subjects within the lifetime of this Investigation. Professor Johnson has therefore had to content himself for the present with an exploratory

survey of the lessons which past experience has to
offer on the questions uppermost in educational discussion today. The skeleton of the more complete
work which the author has in preparation is clearly
indicated, but the elaborations have been confined to
those aspects of the problem which recent educational
discussion has emphasized.

This book owes much to the circumstances under
which it was prepared. Its content is drawn both from
the discussions at the meetings of the Commission and
the material of a course offered by Professor Johnson
at Columbia University on the history of the teaching
of the social sciences, chiefly history. The lectures in
this course were taken down in stenotype and revised
to form this volume without eliminating the vital
spark of active discussion. In this form it is here presented.

The author has here concentrated his attention upon
the longer experience of the old world as this bears
upon the problems of the new. Later studies in this
series by Messrs. Horn, Tryon, and Curti will further amplify the contributions of our own national
experience with certain aspects of the problem of the
social studies.　　　　　　　A. C. KREY, *Chairman.*

CONTENTS

		PAGE
PREFACE		V
CHAPTER		
I.	A QUESTION OF UTILITY	1
II.	HINTS FROM ANTIQUITY	8
III.	FORERUNNERS OF SCHOOL INSTRUCTION IN HISTORY	15
IV.	HISTORY ENTERS THE SCHOOL CURRICULUM	28
V.	"DER KLUGE HOFF-MEISTER"	36
VI.	HISTORY FOR EMILE	48
VII.	JOSEPH PRIESTLEY AS A TEACHER OF HISTORY	61
VIII.	THE TREATMENT OF HISTORY BY BASEDOW AND HIS ASSOCIATES	73
IX.	FREDERICK THE GREAT AS AN ADVOCATE OF SCHOOL INSTRUCTION IN HISTORY	87
X.	KARL MÜLLER'S SURVEY OF HISTORY TEACHING	95
XI.	HISTORY IN THE INTEGRATION OF SCHOOL STUDIES	106
XII.	FITTING THE PAST TO THE PRESENT	119
XIII.	USING THE PAST TO EXPLAIN THE PRESENT	126
	INDEX	137

An Introduction to the History of the Social Sciences in Schools

CHAPTER I

A QUESTION OF UTILITY

If, as any school program in history must imply, it is useful for the young to know something about past human experience, it would appear useful for those who are engaged in shaping history for schools to know something about past human experience with history as a school subject. But to this extension of faith in the utility of past human experience there is the objection that history for schools must be determined by the needs of the present and that those needs are so different from the needs of the past as to render past experience inapplicable. The principle appears so obvious that, in some quarters, any allusion to the past of history teaching is greeted with impatience bordering on contempt.[1] Even

[1] Doctor Abraham Flexner in his book on Universities lists my research course for students interested in the past of history teaching as an "ad hoc" course.

historians, and even historians who hold that history should include all forms of human activity, have been known to frown upon allusions to past activities connected with the teaching of history, and often such allusions have been dismissed with the deadly comment, "What of it?"

This attitude is not new. It was the attitude of the first reformers of history teaching and it has been the usual attitude of reformers of history teaching ever since. To follow the literature left by such reformers is to receive an impression of being always on an educational frontier where everything has a way of beginning at the beginning as if nothing had ever been begun before. On this frontier even the approach to the past through the needs of the present is regarded as new. It was discovered by the earliest advocates of school instruction in history. It has been discovered in every generation since history entered the school curriculum. It is still as new as its youngest discoverer. Yet historically the principle is so old that germs of it may be suspected of having sprouted in the brains of aboriginal men at about the time when memory began to function. It was certainly in operation when the earliest records were written, and it has certainly been in continuous operation ever since. It might, therefore, be cited as evidence that past human experience is not wholly inapplicable to present conditions.

The principle has of late gained fresh momentum from another discovery on the educational frontier—the discovery that we live in a changing world.

Historians for a good many years have been writing about a changing world. Even the old story of the expulsion of Adam and Eve from the garden suggests, in a way, a changing world. Juan Vives, writing on education in 1531, knew that he was writing for a changing world. Everything, he says, has changed, everything changes every day—everything, that is, except human nature, a rather significant exception. Rousseau, writing on education in 1762, knew that he was writing for a changing world and even felt himself "at the edge of a revolution." Education seems for a long time to have been a process of adjustment to a changing world. But on the educational frontier the idea appears to be new, and

3

frontiersmen are only human in thinking that what is new to them must be new to the rest of the world. So we have the new slogan: "Education for a changing world."

That present conditions are different from past conditions is of course freely granted. That history for schools in 1932 must meet conditions in 1932 is of course also freely granted. But if, apart from bringing history down to 1932 and utilizing new material aids such as motion pictures, most of our discoveries about the teaching of history, as may appear in the following pages, are only rediscoveries of ideas exploited, and some of them exploded, in a more or less remote past—what then?

One answer that has come from the lips of living fontiersmen amounts to this: If our discoveries are useful in teaching history now, who cares how many times the same discoveries may have been made in the past? Yet one of the virtues of a "new education" is its newness. In that lies its claim to the magic stamp of "progressive." If the newness is taken away, if it is admitted to be merely a rediscovery, it may of course still be useful, but is it still "progressive"? And if it is of no

4

concern to know whether ideas in education are historically old or historically young, if all that matters is their present utility, why should any one care for further information about ideas in other fields? Why should any one care how anything used to be? Why teach history at all? Can this be mere question-begging as applied to the history that we teach children and sound logic as applied to the history of school instruction in history?

It is admitted of course that the fundamental question is one of utility and not of logic. Is the history of school instruction in history useful? The presumption is against it because it is a history that has not yet been written except in fragments. The sources are widely scattered and few collections of any considerable size have been made. But even such fragments as are now generally available may furnish standards by which to judge progress in the present. Hundreds of experiments alleged to be original and new are now going on in the United States. That they are original with their sponsors may be granted, but it might be useful to test their newness. If, as may appear, some of our most advanced reformers are at best busy catching up with the eighteenth century, that condition might invite useful reflection. And if, as may appear, some eighteenth-century ideas are still useful, there might be a certain economy in taking them out of the eighteenth century instead of taking them out of our own creative energies. There might even be a certain economy in knowing that the nineteenth century abandoned some eighteenth-century ideas which we are now discovering.

Some of the fragments have already been found useful. In Germany it has been declared that some knowledge of the past teaching of history in German schools should be required of those who expect to teach history even in the *Volkschule*. For forty years the field has invited sporadic research in a number of countries, including the United States. When more is written there will be more to say about the utility of the writing. History had been written continuously for twenty-three hundred years before the educational world began to take history seriously as a school subject. Judging by the progress of the last forty years, one may reasonably expect that within a somewhat shorter period the history of school instruction in history will be taken seriously by history teachers and even by reformers of history teaching.[2]

[2] For a brief general sketch of the field and for bibliography, see Johnson, *Teaching of History,* New York, 1915, pp. 86–160 and 439–442.

CHAPTER II

HINTS FROM ANTIQUITY

The oldest history lesson that has come to my attention is in the fourth chapter of Joshua. The twelve tribes of Israel had crossed the Jordan and Joshua had ordered twelve stones set up as a memorial of the crossing. "And he spake unto the children of Israel, saying, When your children shall ask their fathers in time to come, saying, What mean these stones? then ye shall let your children know, saying,"—and the history lesson follows. The objective of the lesson is clearly and definitely stated. It is to inculcate fear of Jehovah.

The procedure is interesting. Observe, in the first place, that the inspiration of the lesson is a current event. Observe, in the second place, that the lesson is not to be forced upon children. It is to be given when children ask for it. It is to be given in response to their "inner urge." It is an illustration of what is now called the "project method" of teaching. Observe, in the third place, that the objective is one that lends itself to immediate realization.

8

Current events, the "project method," and objectives that can be immediately realized—are not all of these of recent discovery? Undoubtedly, and rated as epoch-making. But in the days of Joshua they seem to have been taken as a matter of course. There is, at least, no intimation that Joshua proclaimed himself or was proclaimed as a prophet of a "new education." Nor is there any intimation a thousand years later when the Book of Joshua in its present form was written that the writer thought the lesson in any way remarkable. His only comment is that the stones "are there unto this day." As late as the third century B.C. the principles applied in the lesson appear to have been old. In the twentieth century A.D. they are new.

There are many indications in the Old Testament that the ancient Hebrews used history effectively and some indications that other ancient peoples used history. There was King Ahasuerus on a certain memorable night having history read to him, apparently to induce sleep. "On that night could not the King sleep; and he commanded to bring the book of records of the chronicles, and they were read before the King. And it was found written . . ."

Let those who are looking for examples of history "functioning" in conduct read the sixth chapter in the Book of Esther. Here it is enough to remark that as a direct result of the reading Mordecai was honored and Haman was hanged.

Further evidence of interest in history among ancient peoples is furnished by the stories gathered by Herodotus in his wide travels. Wherever Herodotus went he inquired about things that seemed to him interesting or important and everywhere he made inquiries that called forth stories about the past.

In Herodotus, as in the history lesson in Joshua, the approach to the past is through something that seems interesting or important in the present. In the time of Herodotus it was an old approach. In our time many textbooks in history hold it up as a new approach. It is indeed a part of the conception of the "new history."

"I think," writes Professor Robinson, "that one may find solace and intellectual respose in surrendering all attempts to define history and in conceding that it is the business of the historian to find out anything about mankind in the past which he believes to be interesting or important and about which there are sources of information."[1]

Herodotus wrote his narrative before what is now called "history" had any special name or was regarded by anybody as a separate discipline. He used, it is true, the Greek original of our word "history," but he used it in its then current meaning of inquiry or learning by inquiry. Any kind of inquiry was *historie* and any knowledge obtained by inquiry was *historie*.

Herodotus won his title of "Father of History" not because he was the first to compose what is now called "history" but because he composed it so well that in time *historie* or *historia* took on the restricted meaning of a narrative like that produced by Herodotus, a narrative, that is, of past events.

Herodotus thus had, without striving for it, the kind of solace and intellectual repose which Professor Robinson suggests and found out anything

[1] The *New History*, New York, 1912, p. 73.

that seemed to him interesting or important and about which there were sources of information.

Herodotus appears never to have asked himself, "Is my inquiry useful?" but while he was still at work polishing his narrative his younger contemporary, Thucydides, writing about the Peloponnesian War, introduced a theory of the utility of history. The theory of Thucydides was that "a true picture of events which have happened" may be useful because like events "may be expected to happen hereafter in the order of human things," or as our modern saying has it, "history repeats itself."

After Thucydides, a long line of historians, some of them inspired by Thucydides and some of them by their own reflections, wrote history in the belief that history repeats itself. And a long line of statesmen, generals, princes, philosophers, orators, rhetoricians, and writers read history, believing its "lessons" directly applicable to their own times. History thus became "philosophy teaching by example." It taught by example religion, morals, ideals of life, patriotism. It taught by example what human beings ought to be and to do. And it taught by example what human beings ought not to be or to do.

That history repeats itself is still a wide-spread belief, numbering among its adherents the authors of some of our most "progressive" programs in the "social studies," programs so like other programs which "have happened" before "in the order of human things" that they might themselves be cited in support of the belief. But from scientific history we now learn that history never repeats itself.

The development of didactic history included the writing of some histories that have the flavor of textbooks for the young. Among such works may be mentioned an epitome of universal history, compiled by Cornelius Nepos in the first century B.C.; an epitome of Roman history, compiled by Florus early in the second century A.D. and drawn chiefly from Livy; a compendium of Roman history, compiled by Eutropius in the last half of the fourth century A.D.; and a summary of sacred history compiled by Sulpicius Severus in about the year 403 A.D.

All of these works may have been known to

schoolboys contemporary with them, and all of them were actually used as textbooks after history entered the school curriculum, but indications are lacking that history as a separate study ever figured in school programs in antiquity.

Chapter III

FORERUNNERS OF SCHOOL INSTRUC-
TION IN HISTORY

The Middle Ages produced many historical
works of a didactic character and it is asserted (on
what authority is not indicated) that in many
cloister schools history was zealously taught. It
is admitted, however, that the instruction was
ineffective and that most people had to acquire
their knowledge of history by independent reading.[1]

Among the authors read in the study of Latin
were some Roman historians and through them
doubtless some history filtered into the consciousness of pupils, but I have found no contemporary
evidence that history figured as a separate study
in any school curriculum of the Middle Ages.
Outside of school there may have been a good
deal of history read. From the number of surviv-
ing manuscripts we may conjecture that the work
of Orosius[2] was popular and it seems probable

[1] Hermann Rosenburg, *Methodik des Geschichtsunterrichts, sechste
Auflage*, Breslau, 1910, p. 130.
[2] *Pavli Orisii Historiarum adversum paganos*, completed in 417.

that a work so interesting as that of Gregory of Tours[3] attracted readers. Historians in the Middle Ages certainly showed faith in the utility of history and often expressed it in their prefaces with a profusion of quotations to support them. A fair sample is furnished by Dietrich of Niem in a work completed in 1410. Dietrich, after showing how the ancients felt about history, sums up certain things which seem eminently desirable and concludes, "but these things are to be had only through history."[4]

When we enter the sixteenth century we begin to meet new textbooks in history and specific arguments for school instruction in history. The first of these textbooks was published in 1505[5] and furnishes a striking example of the subordination of history to educational aims. The author was Jacob Wimpheling (1450–1528), scholar, preacher, humanist, reformer, and voluminous writer. The book was the first connected history of Germany that had ever appeared and its pur-

---

[3] *Historia Francorum*, completed about 591.
[4] *Theoderici de Nyem de Scismate Libri Tres*, Leipzig, 1890, pp. 1–6.
[5] *Epitome Rerum Germanicarum usque ad nostra tempora.*

pose was to make young Germans proud of their German past and to stimulate them to enlarge the fame of Germans. This purpose led Wimpheling to take a broad view of history. He wrote of wars and princes but he wrote also of art, literature, inventions, and social customs. He wrote of anything that promoted his purpose, and anything which did not seem to promote his purpose he simply excluded. So severely did he apply this principle that the reader looks in vain in his book for some of the most famous scenes in German history. Take, for example, the struggle between the Emperor Henry IV and Pope Gregory VII. How could any historian of Germany leave that out? Wimpheling could and did.

In what he included Wimpheling found much reason for pride. The Germans were an old people—older than the Romans. The proof was that Rome was founded in 752 B.C. and Trier in 2000 B.C. German achievements in war and in peace were striking. German painting, German sculpture, German architecture, and German literature quite reached the levels of the ancient Greeks. Germans had invented *Bombarden* or *Donner-*

büschen and their invention of printing had given the world as much as the Romans gave when they spread Christianity. Germans were distinguished above all other peoples for hospitality. Germans were more powerful and richer in famous men than any other people.

Wimpheling's patriotism invites comparison with some of our own patriotism. In the introduction to a textbook published in 1898 the author lists, among things which his book is designed to explain, the question, "Why are Americans the bravest men and the most successful of inventors, explorers, authors and scientists? In short, why is the United States the greatest nation in history?"[6]

Wimpheling was a native of old Alsace, born in Schlettstadt, where Germans enlarged their fame in 1870 and reduced it in 1918. It is a matter inviting the comment of the curious that the first connected history of Germany came out of Alsace and that it was a history glowing with German patriotism.

I have found no reference to the actual use of

[6] Ellis, *Young People's History of Our Country*, Boston, 1898, p. vi.

18

the book in schools in the sixteenth century but it appears to have been popular, for it was revised and reprinted as late as the time of Frederick the Great—two hundred and fifty years after its first publication. It was written in Latin but for later editions was translated into German.[7] In patriotism Wimpheling had struck an enduring chord.

In 1524 Luther argued that history should be taught in secondary schools and gave his reasons. Quoting from Varro that, "the best instruction is that which combines illustration and example with precept," Luther showed that history furnishes examples. "There we learn what things those who were pious and wise pursued, what they shunned and how they lived, and how it fared with them, or how they were rewarded, and again how they lived who were wicked and obstinate in their ignorance and what punishments overtook them."

Luther would endow historians as "the most useful of men and the best teachers." But history must be treated critically. It takes the heart of a lion to tell the truth and historians have fallen

[7] See Pavel Viskovatov, *Jacob Wimpheling*, Berlin, 1867, pp. 105–115.

short of the truth. So we must content ourselves with "histories as they are and reflect and judge for ourselves as we peruse them whether the writer has been warped through favor or prejudice, whether he praises or blames either too little or too much. We want the truth in history because the truth will reveal to us the wonderful works of God in the world."

Another idea of Luther's was that in history we see ourselves as in a mirror and thus discover our real selves, an idea of frequent occurrence in the history of history teaching.[8]

Another shining advocate of school instruction in history in the sixteenth century was Juan Luis Vives (1492–1540), Spaniard, scholar, humanist, friend of Erasmus and Sir Thomas More and Henry VIII, before the divorce of Catherine, teacher at Bruges, at Louvain, and at Oxford, author of many books, and now recognized as one of the greatest thinkers of the sixteenth century. Among his works is *De Tradendis Disciplinis* (the transmission of knowledge), a treatise on educa-

[8] H. Keferstein, *Dr. Martin Luther's Pädagogische Schriften*, Langensalza, 1888, pp. 1–3.

20

tion published in 1531, highly regarded in his own century and recently taking rank among the really great treatises on education.

Vives considers history the most excellent of all studies. "Where there is history, children have transferred to them the advantages of old men; where history is absent, old men are as children."

Without history "no one would know anything about his father or ancestors; no one could know his own rights or those of another or how to maintain them; no one would know how his ancestors came to the country he inhabits; no one's possessions would be certain and valid.

"History serves as the example of what we should follow and what we should avoid."

But Vives is fully conscious that he lives in a changing world and allows for it. "Everything," he says, "has changed and is changing every day," except "the essential nature of human beings."

We can know, in spite of changes, "what human passions are, how they are aroused and how quelled, and this" has far more significance than learning "how the ancients built their houses and how they clothed themselves."

"All studies have a connection with one another and a certain affinity," but history seems to occupy a central position. "It is the one study," says Vives, "which either gives birth to or nourishes, develops, cultivates all arts," and he gives examples.

"The medical art is collected from history."

"Moral philosophy is built upon history."

"The whole of law flows out of history."

"A great part of theology is history."

The study of history adds to the joy of living. Children listen with delight to its tales. "Who indeed does not prick up his ears and arouse his mind if he hears anything told which is unusual, great, admirable, beautiful, strong; a noble deed or saying from those stories of which histories are so full?"

There are those who "forget food, drink, and sleep and overcome their natural desires for these necessaries so as to reach the conclusion of the history they are reading."

The course in history which Vives outlined embraces universal history from Adam to his own time and includes a description and keen appraisal of the outstanding historical literature suitable for such a course. Geography is emphasized as essential at every stage of historical study.

In suggesting what should be noted in the study of history, Vives remarks that "wars and battles need not be studied closely, for they merely equip the mind with examples for the performance of evil and show the ways in which we may inflict injuries one on another. . . . Wars should be regarded not otherwise than as cases of theft, as indeed they usually are, excepting perhaps when undertaken against thieves. . . . Let the student then give his attention to peaceful affairs."

The general place which Vives assigns to history may, without violence to his language, be summed up about as follows: History teaches us whence we came, whither we are going, and what we ought to do while we are going.[9]

Johannes Sleidanus (1506–1556) is remembered in standard works of reference as the author of

[9] See *Vives on Education* by Foster Watson, especially pages 231–249. This work contains a translation of the *De Tradendis Disciplinis,* Cambridge University Press, 1913.

the most valuable contemporary history of the times of the Reformation. But another work of his which for a hundred and fifty years made his name a household word in Europe is rarely mentioned. This work was a textbook in history entitled *The Four Monarchies.*[10]

I do not know at what period of his life Sleidanus, or Sleidan, wrote this book, nor the date of its first publication. That for one hundred fifty years it was the reigning textbook in history in Europe is attested by references to it in numerous school programs and by the number of times that it was reprinted. The British Museum has thirteen editions, published at dates ranging from 1559 to 1705. The Union Theological Seminary in New York has an edition of 1557, and Columbia University has a French translation published in 1558. In school programs one often misses the word "history" entirely but finds that the program includes Sleidan. Sleidan seems to have been synonymous with history in about the way that Euclid was so long synonymous with geometry.

10 *De Quattuor Summis Imperiis.*

The title of the book is suggested by a prophecy
in Daniel to the effect that four great monarchies
would arise in the world and that the fourth monarchy would last until the end of the world.
These four monarchies, as Christians interpreted
them, were the Babylonian, the Persian, the
Macedonian, and the Roman. It is a bit difficult
now to carry the continuity of the Roman Empire into the sixteenth century, but it was not
difficult for Sleidan. The Roman Empire, according to the prophecy, was the last of the four monarchies. It was destined to endure while the world
endured, and as the world was still in existence
in the sixteenth century the Roman Empire must
still be in existence. *The Four Monarchies* division of history remained the standard division
until the eighteenth century.

The Four Monarchies thus yielded a principle
of selection and organization. Facts directly related to the four monarchies were included. Facts
not so related were excluded. Yet the book presents in a compact and interesting form (early
editions average about 110 small pages) a fairly

broad view of universal history from the Deluge to Sleidan's own day and contains some bits of what we call social history.

One feature of the work is that for every topic Sleidan indicates his sources. His general attitude seems to be as impartial as it is in his history of the Reformation, and there he is so impartial that his fellow-Protestants disapproved of him.

In the dedication of *The Four Monarchies,* Sleidan places universal history first in a list of valuable studies. At the beginning of his text he remarks on the paucity of sources for the origins of the first monarchy and finds among his authorities wide discrepancies in dates. He has, however, apparently no difficulty in placing the Deluge and gives the date as 1656 years after the creation of the world, and after that feels on secure ground.

The concluding pages of the book leave the reader in the deep gloom of Daniel's prophecy concerning "the fourth and most powerful animal," namely, the Roman Empire. Daniel promises nothing pleasant for the people of God. He promises only horrible persecutions which shall last until the Judgment Day. "The people of God shall be in travail on the whole earth, and the good must suffer while the world endures," and must fortify themselves with such consolation as they can muster against the waves and tempests that threaten them. Thus the book ends.

CHAPTER IV

HISTORY ENTERS THE SCHOOL CURRICULUM

In the cloister school at Ilfeld am Harz, there was established in about 1575 a two years' course in history and geography for the upper classes, with textbooks prepared by the teacher, Michael Neander. The textbook in history (*Compendium Chronikum*) was on the plan of *The Four Monarchies* and brought universal history down to 1575.

The instruction at Ilfeld is interesting for several reasons. In the first place, it may have been the first attempt to teach history as a separate school subject. In the second place, the course was shaped by the needs of pupils preparing for the university. In the third place, Sleidan's *Four Monarchies* was used as a textbook in some universities and may therefore have determined the scope of the instruction at Ilfeld.[1]

[1] Carl Reim in his *Methodik des Geschichtsunterrichts, zweite Auflage,* Halle, 1911, p. 179, says that Neander used Sleidan.

28

Sleidan's book appeared in an English translation in 1563 and in another English translation in 1627, but indications of its use in English schools appear to be lacking. A textbook entitled *Historia Anglorum,* published in England in 1580, has left more definite traces. This book was regarded as so significant that in 1582 a request was presented to the English Privy Council for an order requiring the book to be read in all the schools of England. The argument in favor of this course was that it would make English boys love their country more. The appeal to patriotism won and the Privy Council issued the order. How generally the schools obeyed is difficult to discover, but some schools presumably did obey.

Fifty years later history appeared in the schools of the Oratorians in France and here we meet for the first time special teachers of history. The course included the history of France, sacred history, and the history of Greece and Rome, and was taught throughout in connection with geography. There were textbooks written by members of the Order and special libraries for the use of pupils. The class instruction was oral and was imparted in the French language. Great stress was laid upon the necessity of making the past real to pupils. Pictures, charts, and other aids to visualization were used and teachers described in detail arms, costumes, buildings, and other material conditions of life in the past. History was regarded as of great value in cultivating judgment and in stimulating sound conduct. The mirror idea was prominent. "History is a grand mirror in which we see ourselves. . . . The secret of knowing and judging ourselves rightly is to see ourselves in others, and history can make us the contemporaries of all centuries in all countries."

There was some opposition within the Order to giving history so large a place. One general of the Order, when he wanted to classify a person as mediocre, used to say, "He is a historian." And one member of the Order declared the observation of an insect of greater value than the whole history of Greece and Rome. But such opinions were exceptional.

The educational system of the Oratorians impressed Cardinal Richelieu so favorably that he publicly commended it and in a school which he established in his native town he borrowed its main features, including a course in history.[2]

Comenius (1592–1670), in his *Great Didactic,* completed in 1632, went beyond the Oratorians and proposed a place for history in every grade of instruction from the "school of the mother's knee" up through the university and the "College of Light," an institution for research which was to follow the university. The school system advocated by Comenius embraced a vernacular school with six classes, designed to enroll all children between the ages of six and twelve, and a Latin school with six classes designed to enroll boys of special promise between the ages of twelve and eighteen.

In the vernacular school there was to be a general survey of world history. In the Latin school the course was to be as follows:

Class I—Epitome of Bible History;

Class II—Natural History;

Class III—History of Arts and Inventions;

2 Gabriel Compayré, *Histoire critique des doctrines de l'éducation en France,* I, Paris, 1904, pp. 207–238.

Class IV—History of Morals;

Class V—History of the Customs of Different Peoples;

Class VI—General History of the World and Especially of the Pupils' Own Country.

Here, it is plain, is an arrangement by topics or, to be quite up to date, by "units," with all the topics or "units" brought together in the last year. Moreover, the emphasis is upon what is now called "social history."

Historians had not been writing the kind of history which Comenius had in mind and it would therefore, he said, be necessary to write for each class a special textbook. The treatment must be brief but comprehensive so that no essentials would be omitted. Comenius, that is, had a high regard for history, but he did not mean history in the sense of the standard histories. The divergence thus inaugurated between history in the school and history in histories later became a marked feature of educational discussion of history and has often been carried so far as to suggest that history is a very valuable study until you begin to study some history. You list all the values attributed to history in histories, then you proceed to realize those values through something else.

Comenius imposed upon his history program one important condition. It must be so administered as not to add to the burdens of pupils. Indeed, it must be so administered as actually to lighten the burdens of pupils, a note which has been struck many times since and which may be counted as at least a poor relation of a later discovery that anything in school with any savor of a "task" is reprehensible.[3 and 4]

In Germany history became in the course of the seventeenth century at least a respectable exception in secondary schools and further investigation may show that it was taught in a considerable number of such schools. So far as is now known, however, history was rarely listed as a required study. It was an optional subject and was appar-

[3] See for example the attack upon the "task" idea in *School Review*, Vol. 18, pp. 627–633.
[4] For the ideas of Comenius see *Commenii Magna Didactica*, Leipzig, 1894, especially pp. 213, 222. See also Keatinge's translation. My interpretation differs slightly from Keatinge's.

ently taught outside of the regular program hours. The standard textbook was Sleidan but toward the close of the century a new division of history appeared. Christoph Cellarius (Keller), director of schools in various places, and afterward Professor of History in the University of Halle, divided history into three periods and wrote a book on each, *Historia Antiqua,* published in 1685; *Historia Medii Aevi,* published in 1688; and *Historia Nova,* published in 1696. This division gradually supplanted the *Four Monarchies* division and is of course very familiar to us in our ancient, medieval, and modern history.

In England, John Locke (1632–1704) called history "the mistress of prudence and civil knowledge," and pronounced it a proper study for "a gentleman or man of business in the world." Locke recommended the reading of such historians as Justinius, Eutropius, and Quintus Curtius. "As nothing teaches," he said, "so nothing delights more than history." Yet a large part of the value of history consisted of the horrible examples and warnings found in its pages.[5]

[5] See Locke's *Thoughts on Education,* Cambridge University Press, 1902.

Another English translation of Sleidan's *Four Monarchies* was published in 1661 and may have been used in some English schools in the seventeenth century.

CHAPTER V

"DER KLUGE HOFF–MEISTER"

In 1669 and 1670 two young Saxon counts had
a tutor who has been forgotten by modern com-
pilers of reference works but who in his day was
known as a poet, dramatist, and novelist, and who,
if he were now known to reformers of history
teaching and to teachers of history, might be
quoted in support of some of their most important discoveries. This tutor was Christian Weise
(1642–1708) and the fruit of his tutoring was a
book entitled *Der Kluge Hoff-Meister*.

There is an introduction to the reader in which
Weise regrets that historical studies are for the
most part excluded from the instruction of youth
and that very often it is not until the twentieth
year that a single date is learned. There are still
people who reach the twentieth year in almost
equal innocence of dates, and some years ago
there was talk of writing a history without any
dates in it. Some of us are afraid of dates. Christian Weise was not. In his opinion, any one who

would use history must load his memory with many dates and names, and the time to do this most profitably is before the age of twenty.

"It is claimed," he says, "that history is too difficult for the undeveloped intelligence of youth, but the aim is not to make children accomplished historians. It is simply to lay gradually foundations for later and more mature study."

"Can a child," asks Weise, "learn to know playing cards? Can he distinguish between figures and colors? If so, why can he not just as well grasp a map?"

Similarly, there are games in which children learn very early to count and add. Why then should it seem such a marvelous thing if boys are directed to a few dates? And as for names of countries, cities, and persons, they are as easily acquired as any other words in the vocabulary of children.

Weise has had experience and he knows. He is no armchair philosopher spinning theories. He is spinning his experience with those young counts, and he hopes that his conclusions may be useful to other teachers.

In the body of his treatise he lays down principles and his first principle is that before history can be grasped at all there must be some knowledge of geography. What knowledge, and how shall it be acquired? Weise has a specific answer. All the way along in his treatise he gives recipes that any novice can apply.

He tells exactly how to begin map work. Take a map of Europe, and point out the principal countries—Spain, France, England, Italy, and so forth—and question continuously until after numerous repetitions these are fixed. Then point out the capitals—Paris, London, Madrid, and so forth. And since nothing in a map is clearer or more easily recognized than rivers or coastlines, teach carefully the chief rivers, the Rhine, Rhone, Tiber, and so forth. To make such facts a permanent possession, there must be daily reviews and daily drills. The best way to manage these is to have the pupils ask each other questions, a hint of what is now called the "socialized recitation." In such helpful rivalry, each will try to ask for something that others do not know, and so he will scan the maps and in the process will be strengthening his own memory of the facts. The one to whom the question is put will likewise search the map for the unknown names and in this way gradually become thoroughly acquainted with the map.

After Europe is disposed of, turn to Germany and then add other desired facts. Only observe moderation, and this kind of study will seem more like play than work. It is not necessary to use regular class periods. Have the exercises at mealtimes or at leisure moments.

Many would now dissent from the idea of taking up Europe as a whole first and then coming down to local geography. Many believe that the study of geography should begin with the geography of the schoolyard and gradually work up to the world as a whole, a procedure that often makes trouble for those who wish to begin history in the lower grades. Many times I have been told, "You cannot teach history in the lower grades because the children have not yet had the necessary geography." My own answer is that I can teach the necessary geography as I go along, and often when the regular geography in the course has been the schoolyard I have offended even more than Weise offended. I have begun with a globe map of the world, and, curious as it may appear, I have found that the children got more excited about the world than about the schoolyard. I can understand how Weise's young counts could manage the map of Europe in the manner which he proposes.

Modern pedagogy would object to Weise's drill work as a waste of time and mere drudgery. But those who still believe in drill know the joy that comes to children from a sense of mastery and those who have tried Weise's kind of map drill know that often the problem is not to keep up the interest of children but to stop them when once the exercise is started.

Weise finds dates more troublesome, for however easily children follow out the first hint, it is a long and wearisome road to distinguish clearly one century from another. Weise tells exactly how to begin teaching dates. "It is now," he begins, "the year 1676." Children would know that. "Well, what was last year?" "1675." "What was the year before that?" "1674." So he works back to 1600. "What was the year one hundred years before 1600?" "1500." "A hundred years before 1500?" "1400." Reaching in this way the year 1, Weise calls attention to the birth of Christ, as the event from which we count years.

After this introduction to maps and dates, Weise is ready to begin historical narration. His principle of selection is clear. What history, he asks in effect, should be studied by boys living in Saxony in the year 1676? and answers that history for boys living in Saxony in 1676 must be determined by things that matter in Saxony in 1676, and especially things that matter in the pupil's own community. Weise knows what those things are. He knows, therefore, just what history is needed for boys in Saxony in 1676 and he puts it all into his book, in about 270 pages. It is the history of Saxony plus so much of the history of Germany, Spain, France, England, Denmark, Sweden, Poland, Italy, Turkey, and Switzerland as boys need to understand Saxony in 1676.

Weise has in mind the *Four Monarchies* division but the first three monarchies should, he says, be passed over lightly, and he includes in his book no ancient history. What boys in Saxony need in 1676 is contemporary history and, if you begin with ancient history, the chances are that you will not reach contemporary history.

Weise's principle naturally led him to emphasize current events. He would have his pupils familiar with the *Zeitung*. Evidently there were newspapers in Saxony in 1676. Weise even went so far as to suggest that the ideal way to teach history would be to begin with current events and work backward.

Weise was an advocate of the use of the vernacular in teaching and turns history to account in helping his pupils in their German. Latin, he says, has its proper place for certain people but he who expects to go through the world on Latin will not go far. What every pupil needs is facility in expressing himself in the vernacular, and Weise finds history very useful in loosening the tongues of pupils. To promote this, he would have boys read in turn and read aloud.

Some doubt the value of such exercises in fixing facts, but Weise remarks that in his youth pupils knew all their authors by heart, not because they were required to know them, but simply because of the practice of reading aloud, the understanding being enlightened both through the eye and through the ear.

In emphasizing the need of oral expression and of cultivating the ability to stand up and talk about a thing, Weise refers to the experiences that witnesses have in law courts and shows how the kind of training in expression which he proposes to give through history would enable a witness to face with assurance even the most hostile examiner.

For the further cultivation of oral expression he cites a preceptor he once knew who every evening before prayers in bed had the boys relate something which they had seen in the house, however crude and bungling the result. The next evening they had to write out an account of the same thing and submit the account for criticism. It was a plan which Weise himself had found useful as a preparation for fluent expression in the history lesson.

Weise points out a difficulty which our topical or "unit" plans often render acute. Really to un-

43

derstand history, he says, events must be kept abreast. You follow France for a little while. Then you follow England for a little while. Then you follow Spain for a little while, and then Holland, and then Sweden. In each case you forget what is happening in other countries and you miss the significance of your history. So Weise was a strong advocate of chronological charts with parallel columns to keep things abreast.

The lesson discussion should be friendly and informal. Lead up to the matter gradually: "Listen, tell me what happened to the Augsburg Confession?" or "Listen, tell me how is Martin Luther this morning," always "Tell me"—the personal issue.

This is an interesting point. There are still teachers who think that the way to hold the attention of the class is by the "Tell me" method. That introduces the personal note and if the teacher happens to have a very attractive personality and is, let us say, a beautiful woman teaching a class of high school boys, the boys will be glad to tell her anything. But less attractive teachers are apt to find the personal appeal disappointing and are safer in making the history lesson an affair for the whole class rather than an affair between the pupil who is called upon and the teacher.

Weise has many suggestions on how to question pupils and gives many examples. One of his suggestions is that you should avoid any set kind of questioning. Change the slant or the angle. You ask, for example, When did Charles the Great become Emperor? When did his line die out in Germany? When did Luther propose his discussion of indulgences? When was the Augsburg Confession drawn up? Then you turn the questions around: What happened in 1530? In 912? In 1800? If you stick to just one form or angle of questioning, your class will fall into the state of a simple-minded schoolmaster who could answer very well that "Shem was Noah's son," but to the question, "Who was Shem's father?" had no answer.

Weise would avoid telling pupils anything that they can work out for themselves. "How," you ask, for example, "did the German peace affect the Pope?" Then you give the pupils a chance to answer before you tell them anything about it. Do not rob your pupils of the pleasure of making their own discoveries, but if your pupils are unable to answer, then you must of course tell them.

When a story has been well learned a good deal of discussion may grow out of it. When the boys know the story of the Augsburg Confession, for instance, the teacher may consider what terrible things were urged against the Lutherans, as if they believed in no God and denied the Sacraments; how the Confession gave them a hearing, and how it was translated into other languages. For boys like to hear something new, and the more they know about related conditions and circumstances, the better they will understand the facts under consideration.

Weise recognized, however, that many teachers are lacking in this kind of background and lack the time to acquire it. How often reformers of education meet this obstacle!

Another device of Weise's was to throw history into verse, and he gives some interesting examples. This device has been discovered many times since. Some early American textbooks on history were written in rhyme. A more recent example is Fletcher and Kipling's *History of England,* where Kipling does his part in rhyme. The device was especially popular in the eighteenth century and was then used in rather elaborate textbooks for the use of young children.

Weise closes his discussion with some verses of his own which I have translated literally:

> "A child looks out into the world
>   And learns through the world to know himself;
> For what the flight of time unfolds
> May aptly be called a mirror
> In which man sees his own deeds,
> And what is there contained
> Touches Youth deeply. Who sows such seed
> Will reap in age the harvest."[1]

Verily, *Der Kluge Hoff-Meister* may itself aptly be called a mirror in which we see some of the most fundamental of our own discoveries.

[1] See *Pädagogisches Magazin,* Heft 35, Langensalza, 1893, pp. 1–27. The pedagogical part of *Der Kluge Hoff-Meister* is here reprinted with some extracts from the historical part.

CHAPTER VI

HISTORY FOR EMILE

Jean Jacques Rousseau (1712–1778) in his *Confessions* left a picture of himself which has given him a wide reputation as an "execrable creature." He was probably less execrable than he made himself out to be but indications furnished by other sources suggest at least an unstable character. At the age of sixteen he ran away from an engraver to whom he had been apprenticed, and after that encountered a bewildering variety of experiences, savory and unsavory. He tried many occupations, including plain vagabondage.

In Turin, he found employment as a footman and was dismissed. In Lausanne, he set himself up as a music teacher and failed, partly because he knew scarcely anything about music, and partly because he did not know how to teach music. In Lyons, he became a tutor and failed, partly because he did not like teaching and partly because he did not know how to teach anything.

At the age of thirty, he was in a position to enrich the literature of "How I Lost My Job" if there had then been such a literature.

Later he learned enough about music to write operas and to exert some influence on French music, and when he was fifty he produced *Emile.*

Rousseau mingled with many kinds of society and made many kinds of friends, but he went about with a feeling of being persecuted. He was sensitive and suspicious and most of his friendships ended in quarrels. David Hume, who provided an asylum for Rousseau in England and with whom he quarreled, said that Rousseau was "born without a skin." The most steadfast friends of Rousseau were those who never saw him but were attracted by his writings, beginning with the *Discours sur les Arts et Sciences,* which won a prize offered by the Academy of Dijon in 1749. In this essay Rousseau argued that savagery was preferable to civilization and its publication made him famous.

In 1760, he published *La Nouvelle Heloise,* which proved immensely popular, and in 1762 his

Contrat Social and *Emile,* which brought him to the climax of his fame. But all three of these later works fell under severe criticism, the first on the ground that it was immoral; the second on the ground that its theory of the consent of the governed would undermine monarchy; and the third on the ground that its "Creed of a Savoyard Priest" was bad philosophy and worse religion. *Emile* was condemned by the *Parlement* of Paris and by the Council of Geneva and Rousseau for three or four years seemed to be chiefly occupied in fleeing. He arrived in England early in 1766, but after the quarrel with Hume fled again to France and in 1770 settled in Paris, where for a time he made his living by copying music. He also wrote more books, but all the time he lived in fear of secret enemies. In 1778 he moved to a cottage which a rich man had offered him in the country and there, in the same year, he died.

The central educational doctrine of Rousseau set forth in *Emile* is that education is life and not a preparation for life. "Try to teach the child what is of use to a child and you will find that it takes all of his time." *Emile* was kept from all worry about anything that he would need as a man and given what he needed when his nature seemed to call for it. In carrying out his plan, Rousseau devised a great variety of ingenious "projects," as they would now be called, and the general plan of procedure with Emile might be called "the project method."

History, according to Rousseau, is not one of the subjects that a child needs. Emile is carefully kept away from history until the age of eighteen and Rousseau is severe on "the ridiculous error" of those who think that history should be taught at an earlier age. You can teach children the words of history, but what do the words mean? A child can tell very prettily the story of Alexander swallowing the disagreeable medicine and may even resolve to be an Alexander himself the next time he is called upon to swallow disagreeable medicine, but he misses entirely the real meaning of the story. What is the real meaning? "Poor things!" answers Rousseau. "If you need telling, how can you comprehend it. For Alexander to swallow that draught was to make noble profession of the faith that was in him. Never did mortal man recite a finer creed." And even the boy's tutor did not see that. So why teach the story? (Pp. 74–76.)[1]

Elsewhere in a footnote Rousseau remarks, "The ancient historians are full of opinions which may be useful even if the facts which they present are false. . . . But we do not know how to make any real use of history. Criticism and erudition are our only care, as if it mattered more that a statement were true or false than that we should be able to get a useful lesson from it. A wise man should consider history a tissue of fables whose morals are well adapted to the human heart." (P. 120.)

But Rousseau is equally severe on fables for children. "How can people be so blind as to call fables the child's system of morals, without considering that the child is not only amused by the epilogue, but misled by it? He is attracted by what is false and he misses the truth. . . . Men may be taught by fables. Children require the naked truth." (P. 77.)

[1] The page references in this chapter are to the Foxley translation of *Emile* in *Everyman's Library*.

In an earlier footnote, Rousseau has called attention to the impossibility of using the same words always in the same sense. "I must admit," he says, "that my words are often contradictory but I do not think that there is any contradiction in my ideas." (P. 72.)

Emile meets geography before he meets history. He meets geography with "no book but the world, no teaching but that of fact. The child who reads ceases to think. He only reads. He is acquiring words, not knowledge. . . . You wish to teach this child geography and you provide him with globes, spheres, and maps. . . . What is the use of all these symbols? . . . Begin with the town he lives in and his father's country house, then the places between them, the rivers near them, and then the sun's aspect, and how to find one's way by its aid. . . . Let him make his own map, a very simple map, at first containing only two places. Others may be added from time to time as he is able to estimate their distance and position." (Pp. 131–134.)

At eighteen, Emile is ready for history and needs it. So far, he has been thinking only of himself. Now he is becoming a man, and he must learn to know other men. "Let him see that all men wear almost the same mask. But let him also know that some faces are fairer than the masks that conceal them." The purpose is to teach Emile to read the human heart. Living companions might be chosen for practice, but that would involve the danger of spoiling Emile's own heart. A safer plan is to "show him men from afar, in other times, or in other places, so that he may behold the scene but cannot take part in it."

Even this has its difficulties and dangers. In the first place, history paints the evils of men, rather than the good that they do. It records revolutions and catastrophes. We hear only what is bad. The good is scarcely mentioned. The wicked become famous and the good are laughed at or forgotten. And thus history, like philosophy, slanders humanity.

In the second place, history does not give an exact picture of what really happened. Facts take on color from the interests and prejudices of the historian. "Criticism itself, of which we hear so much, is only the art of guessing, the art of choosing from among several lies the lie that is most like truth."

The accuracy of facts may not matter much, provided the human heart is truly pictured. But here you are apt to encounter the opinions of the historian, and "the worst historians for the young are those who give their opinions." Give the pupil facts, and let him decide for himself. "If he is always directed by the opinion of the author, he is only seeing through the eyes of another, and when those eyes are no longer at his disposal he can see nothing."

Modern history is ruled out because it lacks character and because modern historians think only of highly colored portraits which represent nothing. The old historians show more intelligence, but even among them there is wide scope for choice. Herodotus would perhaps be the best if his details did not run so often to childish folly. Livy is everything which is unsuitable for a youth. Neither Polybius nor Sallust will do, and "Tacitus is the author of the old. Young men cannot understand him." Thucydides is the true model. He relates facts without giving his opinions, but omits no circumstance adapted to make us judge for ourselves. But unfortunately his subject is war.

"History in general is lacking because it only takes note of striking and clearly marked facts, which may be fixed by names, places, and dates, but the slow evolution of facts which cannot be definitely noted in this way still remains unknown.

"Another defect is that history shows us actions, rather than men. It seizes men at chosen times in full dress, when they are prepared to be seen, and describes the clothes of men rather than the men themselves.

"I would prefer," says Rousseau, "to begin the study of the human heart with reading the lives of individuals, for then the man hides himself in vain. The historian follows him everywhere. He never gives him a moment's grace nor any corner where he can escape the piercing eye of the spectator. And when he thinks he is concealing himself, then it is that the writer shows him up most plainly.

"It is true that the genius of men in groups or

nations is very different from the character of the individual man and that we have a very imperfect knowledge of the human heart if we do not also examine it in crowds, but it is none the less true that to judge of men we must study the individual man."

Here, plainly, is the biographical approach to history and this is probably its first appearance in the literature of education.

For biographical material, Rousseau again turns to the ancients, because propriety in modern life no longer permits the details which make biography useful. Plutarch is commended because he abounds in such details and uses them with grace and skill. He gives us the trifles which show what men really were, trifles which modern writers are too grand to tell us anything about. Rousseau also has a good word for Suetonius. "The Lives of Kings," he says, "may be written a hundred times, but to no purpose. We shall never have another Suetonius."

By his reading of the human heart in history, Emile is to be made "wise and good at the expense of those who have gone before." He meets many strange sights in history, but he has already learned to avoid the illusion of passions before they arise and "seeing how in all ages they have blinded men's eyes, he will be forewarned of the way in which they may one day blind his own, should he abandon himself to them." He will not, like young men who study history in the usual way, see himself transformed into the characters he is studying and have the discouragement and regret of finding afterward that he is only himself. Should Emile at any time wish to be any one but himself, even should he wish to be Socrates or Cato, that would prove his whole education a failure. (Pp. 198–202.)

NOTE

In 1916 the Bureau of Education at Washington published a *Report on the Social Studies in Secondary Education*. In it occurs the following passage:

"One principle the Committee[2] has endeavored to keep before it consistently throughout this report because of its fundamental character. It is contained in

[2] Report of the Committee on Social Studies of the Commission on the Reorganization of Secondary Education of the National Education Association, *Bulletin, 1916, No. 28*, Bureau of Education, Washington, D. C., p. 11.

the following quotation from Professor Dewey: 'We are continually uneasy about the things we know and are afraid the child will never learn them unless they are drilled into him by instruction before he has any intellectual use for them. If we could really believe that attending to the needs of present growth would keep the child and teacher alike busy and would also provide the best possible guarantee of the learning needed in the future, transformation of educational ideals might soon be accomplished and other desirable changes would largely take care of themselves.' "

Applied to history this principle is stated in italics: *"The selection of a topic in history and the amount of attention given to it should depend not merely upon its relative proximity in time, nor yet upon its relative present importance from the adult or from a sociological point of view, but also and chiefly upon the degree to which such subjects can be related to the present life interests of the pupil or can be used by him in his present processes of growth."*

"This," according to the Committee, "is a new and most important factor."

It was also new to Rousseau, who on one point was, however, less certain than the Committee.

"A man," says Rousseau, "must know many things which seem useless to a child, but need the child learn, or can he indeed learn all that the man must know? Try to teach the child what is of use to a child, and you will find that it takes all his time. Why urge him to the studies of an age he may never reach, to the neglect of those studies which meet his present needs?

'But,' you ask, 'will it not be too late to learn what he ought to know when the time comes to use it?' I cannot tell, but this I do know: It is impossible to teach it sooner."[3]

[3] *Emile, op. cit.*, 141.

CHAPTER VII

JOSEPH PRIESTLEY AS A TEACHER OF HISTORY

Joseph Priestley (1733–1804), now remembered by general readers who remember him at all chiefly as a chemist who had something to do with oxygen, was in his time a notable figure not only in science but in theology, in philosophy, in politics, and in education. Educated for the Nonconformist pulpit, and called to preach, he advanced, in sermons and pamphlets, ideas which made him an object of suspicion in England. Many regarded him as an enemy of the Church and the King and the feeling against him at last grew so strong that a mob burned his house in Birmingham, burned the meeting-house where he preached, and burned the houses of some of his chief friends and supporters. Continued hostility turned his thoughts to America and the last nine years of his life were spent in America.

In 1761, Priestley was elected a tutor in the classical languages at an academy in Warrington, an academy "for the education of young men of every religious denomination for the Christian ministry or as laymen." To Warrington he went and for six years taught there many things besides the classical languages.

In the course of this experience he produced a *Chart of Biography* which won for him the degree of Doctor of Laws from the University of Edinburgh and *An Essay on a Course of Liberal Education for Civil and Active Life* which entitles him to a place in the history of education.

Priestley found that the educational system of England made no provision for "gentlemen who are designed to fill the principal stations of active life, distinct from those which are adapted to the learned professions," and as a remedy for this defect proposed courses in history and government which he gave at the Warrington Academy and for which he prepared syllabi included in his *Essay*.

The courses were designed for boys of sixteen and seventeen years of age. "It will be said by some that these subjects are too deep and too intricate" for the tender age of such boys, but what, asks Priestley, is there in any of these subjects "which requires more acuteness or comprehension than algebra, geometry, logic, and metaphysics, to which students are generally made to apply at about the same age?"

There were three courses. The first course was "On the Study of History in General and In Its Most Extensive Sense." Its general purpose was "not merely to make history intelligible to persons who may choose to read it for their amusement, but principally to facilitate its subservience to the highest uses to which it can be applied, to contribute to its forming the able statesman and the intelligent and useful citizen." How history in general may serve this general purpose is analyzed in detail in the *Essay* and set forth again in the syllabus of the course. Priestley discusses even the special use of history to ladies.

Priestley's course embraced a full and critical discussion of the sources of history and how to use them, a comprehensive survey of historical literature from Herodotus to Voltaire, and a comprehensive survey of the development of human civilization, including politics, art, literature education, inventions, commerce, social customs, and about everything else that any one can think of as a factor in civilization, with special emphasis upon geography—especially commercial geography—and chemistry as indispensable in the study of history!

The second course was on the history of England from the earliest times to the latest. There is again a very full statement of specific objectives. "The method," says Priestley, "in which I have thought proper to explain the history of England is, to divide the whole into separate periods, and to digest all the materials relating to each under certain important heads." So far as the materials permit, each period or reign of importance is therefore treated under the following heads:

Events.

Religion and Church History.

Government.

> Civil.

> Military.

Officers in the Government.

Peerage.

Parliament.

Constitution, or the balance of power in the several orders of the state.

Laws, including the general state of Law, shewing our gradual removal from a state of barbarism.

Administration of Law, comprising the history of the courts of law.

Feudal System.

Tenures.

    Military.

    Soccage.

Fruits of Tenures.

Descent of Lands.

Alienation of land property.

    Involuntary, with the history of personal execution.

    Voluntary.

    Testamentary.

Entails.

Forms of Conveyance.

Corporations.

Criminal Law.

Trials.

Public Grievances.

Security.
Agriculture.
Mines.
Commodities.
Arts.
Manufactures.
Inland Trade.
Foreign Commerce.
Shipping.
Public Works.
London.
Number of Inhabitants.
Food.
Dress.
Conveniences.

      In Houses.

      Cities.

      Roads, etc.

Language.
Letters.
Learning.
Education.
Manners.
Sentiments.

War.

    Army.

    Navy.

Customs.

Titles, Emblems of Royalty, Court Officials, etc.

Diversions.

Coin, and the Computation of Money.

Price of Provisions.

Revenue.

Taxes, Funds, etc.

Miscellaneous Events.

Great Men Who Flourished in the Period.

Foreign Events.

Let those who have recently discovered that history should be something more than "past politics" commune with Priestley.

The third course is on the laws of England. "It is universally esteemed the disgrace of the English nation," says Priestley, "that the gentlemen and scholars of it are generally so shamefully ignorant of that constitution which is their greatest national glory, and which is regarded with admiration and envy by all foreigners." Government and laws, he points out, have in the past been "considered as the greatest objects of attention which human life affords." And no wonder, "since the happiness of mankind more immediately depends upon them."

The study of them in England "might perhaps contribute more to produce, propagate, and inflame a spirit of patriotism than any other circumstance."

Priestley's *Chart of Biography* has already been mentioned. He compiled also a *Chart of History*. Both are remarkable productions and both were greatly admired in the eighteenth century. They are among the types of aids which I heartily commend to my students and many of these students with the cooperation of their pupils have prepared similar charts and have found them highly illuminating. A part of the *Chart of Biography* is here reproduced. The spelling follows the spelling in the *Chart*.

The method of teaching recommended by Priestley is as follows:

"Let the lecturer have a pretty full text before him, digested with care, containing not only a method of discoursing upon the subjects, but all

A SPECIMEN OF A CHART OF BIOGRAPHY

	Historians &c.
Mirkhond Baronius Hale	
Fitzherbert Coke Montfaucon	
Machiavel Davila Dugdale	
Guiciardin Thuanus Burnet	

	Critics
I. C. Scaliger Vossius Rollin	
W. Lilly Casaubon Temple	
Politian Turnebus Selden Bently	

	Poets &c.
Ariosto Malherbe Boileau	
Holbein Shakespeare Dryden	
Raphael Tasso Milton Pope	
Titian Poussin Handel	

	Mathemat. &c.
Paracelsus Harvey Boerhaave	
Copernicus Ld. Bacon Newton	
Cardan Descartes Hans Sloan	
C. Agrippa T. Brahe Boyle Maclaurin	

	Divines &c.
Calvin Pascal Shaftesbury	
Luther Grotius Le Clerc	
Erasmus Arminius Tillotson	
Beza Locke	

	Statesmen
Francis 1st Cromwel Peter Gr.	
Columbus Philip 2d Turenne Charles 12th	
Albuquerque Henry 4th Lewis 14th	
Charles 5th Richlieu Marlborough	

Scale: 50 — 1500 — 50 — 1600 — 50 — 1700 — 50

69

the principal arguments he adduces, and all the leading facts he makes use of to support his hypotheses. Let this text be the subject of a regular, but familiar discourse, not exceeding an hour at a time; with a class not exceeding twenty, or thirty. Let the lecturer give his pupils all encouragement to enter occasionally into the conversation, by proposing queries, or making any objections or remarks which may occur to them. Let all the students have an opportunity of perusing this text, if not of copying it, in the intervals between the lectures, and let near half of the time for lecturing be spent in receiving from the students a minute account of the particulars of the preceding lecture, and in explaining any difficulties they might have met with in it; in order that no subject be quitted, till the tutor be morally certain his pupils thoroughly understand it.

"Upon every subject of importance, let the tutor make references to the principal authors who have treated of it; and if the subject be a controverted one, let him refer to books written on both sides of the question. Of these references, let the tutor occasionally require an account, and sometimes a written abstract. Lastly, let the tutor select a proper number of the most important questions which can arise from the subject of the lectures, and let them be proposed to the students as exercises. . . .

"Some may object to the encouragement I would give the students to propose objections at the time of lecturing. This custom, they may say, will tend to interrupt the course of the lecture, and promote a spirit of impertinence and conceit in young persons. I answer, that every inconvenience of this kind may be obviated by the manner in which a tutor delivers himself in lecturing. . . .

"But suppose a lecturer should not be able immediately to give a satisfactory answer to an objection, which might be started by a sensible student. A tutor must be conscious of his having made very ridiculous pretensions, and having given himself improper airs, if it gives him any pain to tell his class, that he will reconsider a subject; or even to acknowledge himself mistaken. . . . For my own part, I would not forego the pleasure and advantage which accrue, both to my pupils and to myself, from this method, together with the opportunity it gives me of improving my lectures, by means of the many useful hints which are often started in this familiar way of discoursing upon a subject."

Priestley actually gave his courses to boys of sixteen and seventeen and gave them successfully, believing that thus, "instead of barren heads, barbarian pedants, wrangling sons of pride, and truth-perplexing metaphysic wits, men, patriots, chiefs, and citizens are formed."[1]

[1] I have used for this account the *Essay* as published in London, 1765. See also T. E. Thorpe, *Joseph Priestley,* London, 1906.

CHAPTER VIII

THE TREATMENT OF HISTORY BY BASEDOW AND HIS ASSOCIATES

Johann Bernhard Basedow (1723–1790) is a striking illustration of how unpleasant personal experiences may make reformers. In the first place, his home life as a child was very unhappy. His mother was melancholy and eventually became insane. His father was severe to the point of brutality. As a little boy, Johann disliked school. He disliked still more collecting and delivering wigs after school hours. His father's trade was the making and cleaning of wigs and Johann was expected to follow the same trade, but at the age of eighteen he ran away from home and found shelter in the family of a physician who was impressed by the appearance of talent in the young man, and eventually convinced the father that Johann would make a good minister of the gospel. So Johann was sent to the gymnasium in Hamburg and finished the course there, after a fashion, his teachers, with one exception, reporting that he did not seem to know anything about anything. He had been exposed to the system but the system had failed to take. The effect on Basedow was that he disapproved of the system. He thought that there must be something wrong with the system. It never occurred to him that there might be something wrong with Basedow.

In one field Basedow made progress. At the age of twenty-three, he wrote a poem of one hundred stanzas proving how indispensable a knowledge of history is to right living, and in 1752 he wrote a dissertation in which he developed ideas very similar to those which ten years later appeared in Rousseau's *Emile*.

Basedow went to the University of Leipzig where, after sampling the professors and disapproving of them, he collected some books and proceeded to acquire a university education in his own room. He had associations with other students in beer gardens and in other forms of extra-curricular activities, and these he seemed to enjoy. But he emerged from his university course with a conviction that the whole system of education needed reconstruction.

74

Basedow began by attacking violently the existing system and its leaders. His psychology seems to have been excellent. He seems to have felt that, though he might be damned all over Europe for his attacks upon respectable figures, that would be good advertising and would eventually gain a hearing for his ideas, and it did. The noise of his publicity attracted the attention even of kings and empresses. He had to his credit some teaching experience. He had been for three years the tutor of a young boy, and, according to Basedow's report, this boy made very remarkable progress. Basedow announced that he had discovered a new method of teaching by which any one would make remarkable progress. He could teach language by this new method. He could teach history by this new method. He could teach anything by this new method. His pupils by the age of twelve would know more than most adults in Europe at any age. They would know more about religion than even ministers of the Gospel. All this must have been true, because Basedow himself kept admitting it.

He was a prolific writer. He published some

ninety-one works in the course of his life. His interest embraced the whole field of education and he made solid contributions, some of them so far in advance of his time that we have scarcely yet caught up with them. His *Elementarwerk* brought together materials of instruction for use in the elementary school, and he compiled textbooks for secondary schools, among them textbooks in history. He had the courage of his convictions. Witness in his *Elementarwerk* a chapter on sex hygiene which made ministers and others blush. He established an institute at Dessau which drew pupils from several European countries and many visitors who carried away his ideas. He was a power in education, in the latter half of the eighteenth century. A part of his prestige came from an impression that he was applying the ideas of Rousseau's *Emile,* and he was, but he had independently arrived at similar ideas in his dissertation of 1752.

In this dissertation Basedow advocated teaching history backwards as the first stage in historical instruction. In this way he proposed to present the history of the great empires. Beginning with the Holy Roman Empire, he would have pupils move backwards to the Byzantine Empire, then to the Roman, then to the Greek, then to the Persian, and so on back to the "obscure traditions" of the Deluge. After this world survey, he would have Old and New Testament history and end with an exposition of the Lutheran Catechism.

Basedow looked to history for what is directly useful, and history seemed to him useful chiefly as a collection of examples, examples to imitate, and examples to shun. In the ancient history which he abridged from standard ancient historians with slight changes, horrible examples overshadowed the good. The salacious gossip of Suetonius, for example, is repeated for the edification of boys in their teens. It is not until he reaches Caligula that Basedow begins to have qualms.[1]

In his *Methodenbuch,* first published in 1770, Basedow shows how history may be adapted to highly specialized needs. He devotes a whole chapter to history for a prince. For a prince, it is

[1] *Historiæ Antiquæ Liber VIII. Primorum Cæsarum XII Vitæ. Auctore C. Suetonius Tranquillo. Utiliter Breviate et in Paucis Mutato.*

fundamentally important to study the history of his own country but not in the form in which ordinary textbooks present it. The needs of a prince are so different from the needs of his subjects that he must have a special treatise written exclusively for princes. It should contain, first, a chronological survey and then a special treatment of such topics as:

(1) History of remarkable revolutions.

(2) History of changes in law and politics.

(3) History of population and finance.

(4) History of diplomacy.

(5) History of the morals of reigning houses.

This topic is enforced by examples, a partial list of which follows:

(*a*) Examples of striking industry and striking laziness on the part of rulers and the consequences.

(*b*) Examples of misers and spendthrifts among rulers and the consequences.

(*c*) Avoidable and unavoidable causes of national debt.

(*d*) Examples of how avoidable and injurious wars were brought about.

(*e*) Examples of special bravery on the part of princes and others.

(*f*) Instructive history of favorites.

(*g*) Instructive history of mistresses.

(*h*) Examples of cruelty, if such there be, with their consequences.

(*i*) Examples of the ingratitude of princes, if such there be, toward faithful servants, and the consequences.

(*j*) Examples of intolerance with judgments upon them.

(*k*) Examples of the influence of the clergy upon the state and upon princes.

Every topic is selected with special reference to the particular needs of a prince, and some of the topics, it is clear, would not be suitable for the subjects of a prince.

The writing of such a history would require the work of two men for several years. The first must be familiar with archives and be able to present to the second useful anecdotes. The second must be a philosophic friend of humanity and a master of the art of writing. But—and this was very important—the book must not be printed. It would never do to let the subjects of the prince know the kind of history that a prince studied. The book must be kept in manuscript and used only in the secrecy of the council chamber. In that secrecy the prince must learn the book very thoroughly.[2]

For general school purposes, Basedow proposed some incidental teaching of historical facts in the lower classes, and, beginning with boys of fifteen, a sketch of universal history. Examples of virtue and of vice are again emphasized, but they are examples suitable for the subjects of princes. The instruction is to be so pleasant as to seem more like play than study.

At Dessau there was little memorizing and what there was was of an easy sort. Pupils were expected to retain a general impression that human beings, families, and peoples had lived long ago, as now, under a variety of states. Differences are emphasized, and here Basedow shows that he had some historical sense. Only by appreciating differences between past and present would pupils be able to place themselves in their own time.

[2] *Methodenbuch,* edition of 1770; the chapter is omitted from later editions.

Basedow had little to say of patriotism and did not include in his course German history. "Our aim," he says, "is to make our pupils Europeans rather than Austrians or Saxons, that is, to make them men first and then citizens." This attitude was due in part to the cosmopolitanism of the eighteenth century and in part to the number of different countries from which pupils came to Dessau. Basedow did, however, favor celebrations of national festivals and spoke with approval of the drama as an instrument for the cultivation of patriotism.

Diligently as Basedow sought for things useful in themselves, he held that a textbook must not leave the pupil ignorant of names and things found mentioned in all writings, or of which ignorance might be bad, even if this knowledge is not in itself useful. Mythology, genealogy, and heraldry should therefore be included.

Basedow believed that history should be made as real as possible. With great labor and great care he had engravings made to illustrate history. His fundamental principle was that every picture must be as accurate and authentic as the text itself and that must be very accurate. Basedow recognized, however, the difficulty of telling the truth in a textbook. "All existing books," he says, "have errors and doubtful statements. The textbook writer simply borrows from other writers. Sometimes his judgment is erroneous. Sometimes he is careless. Sometimes he gives the facts but puts a wrong interpretation on them. Sometimes the printer makes mistakes, and it would be the greatest wonder in the world if a textbook should be wholly true." But it must be as accurate as possible.

Christian Ernst Trapp (1745–1818) was a teacher with Basedow at Dessau and later a professor of pedagogy in the University of Halle. At Dessau Trapp excited some comment by objecting to the use of the Priestley charts, copies of which had been brought to Dessau by its prince. Trapp thought that it was better for pupils to make their own charts. Trapp had other ideas of his own. He believed in correlating history with geography and Latin. He observed that the older historians furnished better models of writing than the textbook writers of the day. So in his classes he used the old historians. He introduced note-books much like the workbooks which are flood-ing the United States now. He encouraged his pupils to see that in writing up their notebooks they were really writing history. He laid great stress on current events. But the most striking thing in Trapp's experience at Dessau was his use of what is now called the "true and false" method of testing. The class in history stood in a row just as some of us used to stand when we were "spell-ing down." Trapp would read a sentence and then all the pupils who thought it a true statement would hold up both hands above their heads. All who thought it a false statement would leave their hands hanging down by their sides. All who were in doubt about it would put out their hands hori-zontally. That made checking easy.

Here are some of the sentences that Trapp read:

"Cyrus lived before Abraham." Two sets of hands went up.

"Demosthenes and Cicero were orators and were associated in Athens." Four pupils raised their hands.

"Socrates was a friend and teacher of virtue but

Alexander, Philip's son, King of Macedonia, was more amiable than he." Most of the class stretched out their hands horizontally.

"Luther and Calvin were at one time famous schoolteachers." Results not recorded.

As a teacher Trapp was voted a failure both at Dessau and at Halle. He could think better than he could teach and found his right vocation when he became editor of an educational journal.

Joachim Heinrich Campe (1746–1818) was for a few months Basedow's successor at Dessau. After that, he founded, in succession, two institutions of his own, both of which came to an early end through difficulties with the Church. After that, Campe became the editor of an educational journal and engaged in other literary work. He wrote many books for children, among them a book on ancient history in verse, accompanied by pictures. His most significant discovery was the place of the saga in the teaching of history. In this he seemed dimly conscious of the culture epoch theory, the theory that the individual in his mental experience repeats the experience of the race. The saga being among the earliest forms of human history seemed for that reason adapted to young children.

C. G. Salzmann (1744–1811) was a minister called to Dessau to direct the devotional exercises of the school, but he became interested in the general scheme and in 1784 founded a school of the same kind at Schnepfenthal. Here he developed the community approach to history.

His criticism of current programs sounds quite familiar in the twentieth century. "History," he says, "as it is ordinarily taught lifts the pupil out of the society of the living and places him in the society of the dead." The pupil learns what happened a thousand years ago without learning what is happening now. He is taught to admire the wonders of Athens, Rome, and Sparta, their wars, their buildings, their art, yes, even the tales of Venus and Cupid, without knowing what assemblies, mayors, and the like really are. He is taught to prattle about consuls, tribunes, and dictators. He is taken to visit in imagination the Forum and the Areopagus, without ever seeing with his eyes the inside of his own city hall. So here in Schnepfenthal, let us study the history of Schnepfenthal.

After we get acquainted with our own community, then we can go out and get acquainted with some neighboring communities, and after awhile we can pick up a book and read something about distant communities, especially if we keep up our geography.

Salzmann, in disagreement with Basedow, would exclude mythology. The ancient gods, he said, were not only immoral, they were pure unreason, and nobody would take any of them seriously except for the poets and artists who had made them beautiful.

Erudition in any field seemed to Salzmann unnecessary for teachers. Teachers should study children.[3]

[3] For the ground covered by this chapter there is a large mass of literature. See especially Julius Gallandt, *Ein Beitrag zur Geschichte des Geschichts-Unterrichts im Zeitalter der deutschen Aufklärung;* Berlin, 1900; R. Diestelmann, *Basedow,* Leipzig, 1897; and A. Pinloche, *L'Éducation en Allemagne,* Paris, 1889.

CHAPTER IX

FREDERICK THE GREAT AS AN AD-VOCATE OF SCHOOL INSTRUCTION IN HISTORY

Frederick the Great (1712–1786) ascended the throne in 1740 and reigned in what has been called the "golden age of German pedagogy." Frederick was himself a part of the gold. His advice to pedagogues is as great in its way as his military achievements and statesmanship.

Born in an atmosphere where every man did his "verdammte" duty, Frederick from his earliest years was expected to do his duty as his father, Frederick William I, saw it.

The father had definite ideas about education and devised an eminently practical system for his son. He saw no use in Latin and strictly excluded it from his list of studies. But Frederick's mother and his governess and first tutor applied surreptitiously a different theory, and Frederick thus acquired an excellent knowledge of French and a taste for literature and music and even managed to learn a little Latin. Hints of this kind of progress reaching his father brought Frederick under discipline so harsh that at the age of eighteen Frederick tried to run away. His experience in a way had been as unpleasant as Basedow's experience and prompted a similar escape. But Frederick's plan was discovered and he was imprisoned for fifteen months in a fortress. Then he made peace with his father, married a German princess selected by his father, and lived happily for seven years on an estate given him by his father, performing the duties of his position to the satisfaction of his father, and yet indulging his tastes for literature.

He was most at home in French. In fact, he habitually spoke and wrote French, and one of his ambitions was to be considered a great French author. German seemed to him a language fit only for boors. He predicted, however, in French, of course, a great future for German literature and actually lived into the era of Kant and Goethe and Schiller without discovering the fulfilment of his prophecy.

Frederick began early to observe the kind of

education which packs the minds of children with facts, giving them merely something to remember, and protested that this was not education at all. The important thing in education was the use of reason. He had arrived at this conception before he mounted the throne and he soon began his attempts to turn education in Prussia in that direction, culminating in his famous school regulation of 1763, making education compulsory between the ages of five and fourteen. Later, secondary and higher education received his attention.

History held a high place in the educational thinking of Frederick the Great. His general argument is summed up in his *Memoirs of the House of Brandenburg*. "History," he there points out, "is looked upon as the school of princes. It exhibits to their memory the reigns of sovereigns who were fathers of their country, and of those tyrants who laid it waste. It points out the causes of the increase and decline of empires. It displays such a multitude of characters that some of them cannot help bearing a resemblance to those of the princes of our days, and while it decides the reputation of the dead, it pronounces a tacit sentence on the living. Thus the censure which history passes on those wicked men who are no more is a moral lesson to the present generation by which they are given to understand what kind of judgment posterity will form of their conduct.

"Though the study of history is of all others the most proper for princes, yet it is not less useful to private persons. . . . Here the civilian, the politician, and the soldier learn the connection of things present with the past; here they find encomiums bestowed on those who faithfully served their country and universal odium entailed on the names of such as abused the confidence of their fellow citizens; here, in fine, they are made wise by the experience of others.

"To contract the sphere of our ideas to the spot we live on, or to confine our knowledge to our private duties is to grovel in the most stupid ignorance. But to penetrate into the remote recesses of antiquity, to comprehend the whole universe within the extent of the mind is really to triumph over ignorance and error, is to co-exist with all ages, and to become a citizen of all places and countries."[1]

Frederick did more than argue for history. He wrote history. Seven of the thirty volumes of his collected works as published in 1846–1857 are historical. And he outlined school programs in history. In his instructions for the direction of the Academy for Nobles in Berlin, he advocates modern history, and especially the history of the fatherland. He is a champion of the truth. Elsewhere he says that if historians write without liberty to tell the truth their work can be only mediocre, or positively bad, and that one ought to respect less the memories of the dead than truth, which never dies. But Frederick believed that the truth should be made to preach. There must be examples of heroism to inspire pupils. The teacher must strive to bring out the moral of the lesson. In teaching the Crusades he must preach against superstition. In teaching the night of St. Bartholomew he must preach against fanaticism. Every good deed must have its meed of praise and its implication, "Do thou likewise." The pupil must see constantly

[1]See English translation, Robertsons, Edinburgh, 1759, pp. 1–2.

that without goodness there can be neither fame nor true greatness.

Frederick's call upon teachers of history to preach is interesting. It is in striking contrast to the idea of Rousseau, "Give the facts and let the facts produce their own impression." But the eighteenth century had more teachers of history who used history for preaching than the kind of teachers suggested by Rousseau. The nineteenth century kept up this kind of preaching and many history textbooks were published which were in effect collections of sermons. Authors consistently preached. In the 90's the moral began to disappear, but in our own time teachers of history are again being admonished to preach and preaching textbooks in history are again being produced.

In his *History of My Own Time,* Frederick is rather severe in his criticism of professors of history. He quarrels with the investigators of his day for devoting so much attention to trifles, and calls for more effort to distinguish between essentials and non-essentials. "Is it a mortal sin," he asks, "to fall into error as to the exact date of the death of Belus or as to the exact day on which Darius' horse lifted his master to the Persian throne, or as to the hour at which the *Golden Bull* was published, whether six in the morning or seven in the evening? For my part," he adds, "I am content to know what the *Golden Bull* contains and that it was promulgated in 1356."

He then admonishes the historian to put into history only what is essential.

Frederick gave specific directions for the teaching of German history. The obscure beginnings were to be passed over briefly with mention of only a few of the most important events before the thirteenth century. From the thirteenth century on, there should be a fuller and larger study, and on reaching modern times, still more detail, with careful attention to life in the present.

Here Frederick is obviously in agreement with our modern prescription: Compress the ancient world, bring out only essentials that have a bearing on life now, abridge the Middle Ages, and expand the strictly modern period, especially contemporary history. In one respect he differed, and that was in thinking that political history was still important. This was at a time when textbooks in history were responding to a new enthusiasm for *Kulturgeschichte,* and tending to minimize political history. Frederick the Great believed in *Kulturgeschichte,* but included political history as an essential part of *Kulturgeschichte.*[2]

[2] Frederick made frequent references to the teaching of history. See especially *Tome VII* of his collected works.

CHAPTER X

KARL MÜLLER'S SURVEY OF HISTORY TEACHING

Several special treatises on the teaching of history appeared in the eighteenth century and at least a dozen appeared in the first quarter of the nineteenth century. Each of them announced about the same discoveries and in each case the discoveries were announced as if they were original. Each of them, like *Der Kluge Hoff-Meister* in the seventeenth century, apparently grew out of the personal experience and inner consciousness of the author. In each case the author might have asked, "Who cares what history used to be taught or why or how?" and answered, "I am writing about the history that should be taught now, and why, and how."

Karl August Müller may not have been the first to take history so seriously that he actually used history in writing about the teaching of history, but he is the first with whom I happen to be acquainted.

Müller was a teacher of history in Dresden and

his book was published in Dresden in 1835. In the preface the author states that he has been a student of history, that he has had a varied experience as a teacher of history, and that he has made a diligent use of the experiences of others.

The range of his acquaintance with earlier writings is indicated by an annotated bibliography. The annotations are very frank. One author he pronounces "trivial and confused." Another "says in barbarous language insignificant things." From another he quotes, "The author so far as he remembers has read no pedagogical work except Rousseau's *Emile* and on methods of teaching only what Gaspari has written in his *Methods of Teaching Geography*." Müller's comment is, "No one can be such a fortunate genius as to evolve all wisdom out of himself."

The bibliography is far from complete. It is confined to special treatises on the study and teaching of history and within this field is confined to treatises whose titles openly proclaim their character. Titles that have a general educational flavor even when, as in the case of Weise's *Kluge Hoff-Meister* and Priestley's *Essay on Edu-*

cation, they conceal special treatises on the teaching of history, are consistently ignored.

Müller begins with a discussion of the *Wesen Werth und Zweck des Historischen Studiums.* The word *"Wesen"* invites comment. Few historians before the nineteenth century worried about this *"Wesen."* History was simply one of those words the meaning of which was clear to everybody and only when people began to ask, "What is history?" was it discovered that nobody really knew, and that the more they thought about it the less they seemed to know. Müller knew at least what history meant to Müller.

Approaching the value of historical study, Müller remarks that nothing can be more futile for a teacher than to talk about the value of his subject because those who understand the subject will understand its value without any talk about it and those who do not understand the subject will not understand talk about the value of the subject.

Müller was evidently something of a scholar and may have been writing for scholars. He quotes in Greek, Latin, French, and English without translating a single word of his quotations into German. This taint of scholarship should no doubt be considered by those who argue that scholarship has been an injury to education.

Müller found one other objection to talk about the value of history. So much had already been written that no one could hope to say anything new. That is one of the handicaps imposed by a little knowledge of what was written before we were born. It is an illustration of how history may take the joy out of living and hamper our creative powers.

But in spite of this handicap Müller was able to see clearly that history teachers in the schools of his time were "utterly without principles, without plans, and without purposes." Our whole régime of secondary education is today drawing about the same criticism.

In the face of an actual situation as he saw it, Müller did his duty. After pointing out the consequences of teaching history without principles, plans, or purposes, he analyzes the social conditions of his time, finds what society needs, and then shows what history can do to meet these needs. It is a very detailed analysis. It takes up all the activities of his time and shows that no activity has any meaning apart from history. It takes up the other subjects of study one by one and shows that no study has any meaning apart from history. Always, you need history to give a meaning to things. You need history to keep superstition out of religion, to avoid waste of effort in art, and wasted effort in all kinds of human activity. You need to build upon the past experience of the race. But statesmen have not been doing it. Generals have not been doing it. Artists have not been doing it. Teachers have not been doing it. Let us now do it and have a very different world. Müller flames into eloquence over the possibilities.

Becoming somewhat more specific, Müller finds that the chief aim of instruction of any kind is to develop the human in us, to develop, that is, the things in our physical and mental makeup which differentiate us from the lower animals, and here history is the most useful of all studies, or would be if history were not ruined by wretched teaching. It has greater possibilities than either the classics or mathematics in introducing children to life, to society, to the best and noblest of our race, and to the best and noblest of humanity. It is an indispensable study for all kinds of pupils in all grades of instruction.

Müller does not worry much about special methods of teaching. "Method," he says, "is something that you carry about inside of you. It is your spirit that you make living. Only let your spirit reveal itself as it can and will and it will awaken other spirits." That is the main thing in teaching. But there are certain fundamental principles to consider. "Order your entire history plan so that one part supports another, and so that in a graded series you pass from one thing to another throughout the course. The whole course must be viewed as a unit and every part of it must be planned with reference to the whole unit. The work in each class must be a natural sequence of work in the preceding class and must fit into the next year's work. At the same time it must be so arranged as to furnish the best preparation that can be thought of for those pupils who have only that one year's work."

Program makers as far back as the seventeenth century had glimpses of this principle, but Müller saw it clearly and worked out in detail its implications. How far his influence extended, I do not know, but the principle grew to be an axiom for Continental Europe and, except in England and the United States, is today a commonplace in discussions of history programs.

Historical instruction, according to Müller, should proceed from the particular to the general and from the general to the whole. This is justified on psychological grounds. Not too much abstraction, not too much generalization, but such as there is must proceed from the particular to the general. Do not lay down the general and then bring in the particular to illustrate. Begin with whatever is nearest to the circle of ideas in your pupils and can most easily be related to those ideas. There is here a kind of emphasis on the pupils' immediate surroundings that you get in Salzmann. Müller does not mention Salzmann anywhere but, of course, if you begin with a study of the pupil's own direct experiences you are going to utilize anything that he has in his own immediate community.

Historical instruction, according to Müller, should have in mind humanity as a whole and not some special phase of humanity or human development. This is enlarged upon. Müller shows what happens if history is taken up piecemeal in the form of topics or units and concludes that such treatment cannot lead to a real understanding of history. It is all right, of course, to treat special phases of history, but this should always be done from the point of view of humanity as a whole. Always, says Müller, keep that in your eye.

History, according to Müller, should be brought into close relations with other studies. Utilize in your teaching every other study that the pupils are taking parallel with it, and as opportunities arise in the teaching of history, apply your history. Run it out into all of the other fields. If ever there was a good teacher of history, either before or after Müller, who failed to apply this principle I have never found the evidence.

The time and place relations are essential. Müller takes strong ground against those who think that history can be taught without chronology or geography.

Applying his principles to a program, Müller works out two cycles, with hints of what later came to be called "concentric circles." He proposes to begin with children of nine, but he outlines work for earlier stages, consisting of myths, sagas, and biographies. Both cycles have ancient history followed by German history down to 1835, but in the second cycle pupils are made conscious of sources and elementary historical criticism, and Müller calls this part of the course an introduction to the study of history. He does not go so far in this direction as Priestley went, but he recognizes clearly the need of arousing consciousness of the historical method of arriving at truth.

Müller devotes sixteen pages to the preparation, training, and outlook of the history teacher. In the first place, the history teacher must be a man of the finest character. Any one else is ruled out. He must be orthodox in religion. That is fundamental. In addition to these qualifications, the teacher of history must know what historical research is. He must know what the primary sources of history are, and the sort of thing that comes out of primary sources for a teacher. He must have a wide acquaintance with historical literature, and it is desirable that he should also be a writer of history. Then, he must know his pupils, so that his teaching all the way through is determined by two considerations: scholarship and the mental abilities of his pupils. But in adapting history to the mental abilities of his pupils he must carefully avoid doing any violence to the integrity of historical scholarship. He must teach the truth about the past.

Is teaching the truth a safe procedure? Here are heroes who have been idealized. The teacher tells the truth about them. Some descendant of a hero, it may be, is at the moment sitting on the throne. What will he do to you if you tell the truth about his ancestors? Müller has a device for avoiding danger, which when summed up amounts to this: Keep right on teaching the truth, but teach it with discretion.

In Müller's time, as in ours, the market was filled with textbooks and Müller has a recipe for using textbooks. And he does not hesitate to name the textbooks which seem to him the best. That must have taken courage beyond discretion.

Müller has in view chiefly secondary schools but he turns aside to argue that history should be a required study in the *Volkschule* (at that time history was optional in the *Volkschule*) and he outlines national history with a little smattering of information about other peoples at the end of the course. The idea of the world whole, he says, cannot be applied in the *Volkschule*.

Müller wants more time for history in secondary schools. He wants a minimum of three hours a week instead of the usual two hours and for the work of the first year he wants six hours a week. Give us more time, he says, in effect. Give us better-trained teachers. Give us the kind of history that I am advocating and you shall soon see what history in school is good for.[1]

[1] Karl August Müller, *Ueber den Geschichtsunterricht auf Schulen*. Dresden, 1835.

CHAPTER XI

HISTORY IN THE INTEGRATION OF SCHOOL STUDIES

When, about one hundred years after Herodotus, and thanks to his influence, history became differentiated from knowledge in general, there remained a recognition of its relations to other branches of learning. The earth, as the theatre of events, could not be ignored. Historians at the very least had to take account of the place relation of events and this often led to detailed geographical descriptions. As far back as Hecatæus, there was also some appreciation of geographic influence. Hecatæus called Egypt "the gift of the Nile," and Herodotus, who is usually regarded as the author of the phrase, agreed with Hecatæus.

History as a branch of literature remained in the family of literature. History as "past politics" had associations with present politics. History as philosophy teaching by example was closely connected with morals. History as the revelation of God's purpose in the world was a part of religion. History as the sum of what man had thought and achieved in the world had relations with every branch of human learning, and there was a time when one of the qualifications prescribed for writing history was a knowledge of all branches of learning.

The earliest advocates of school instruction in history were conscious of such relations and writers on the teaching of history down to the present have habitually emphasized them. Indeed, as early as the sixteenth century there were writers so impressed by such relations that they were led to attempt a fusion of history with other studies. In 1561, for example, Franciscus Balduinus published a work entitled *De Institutione Histoiriæ Universæ et ejus cum Jurisprudentia conjunctione,* in which he undertook to fuse history with something like what is now called political science. The work seems to have been received with some acclaim and was reprinted in 1728. The title certainly breathes fusion and the first few pages breathe fusion. But what the writer really does is to discuss the utility of history in the usual sixteenth-century way, with bits of pious *obiter dicta* scattered along the way about history *cum Jurisprudentia conjunctione*. The reader begins with enthusiasm and at the end of the book feels that he has been deceived. Many writers since the days of Balduinus have unfurled the flag of fusion with a zest equal to his and at the end have left the reader with a feeling of having been deceived.

In the seventeenth century the relations between history and other studies suggested conscious correlation and Christian Weise applied the principle with a high degree of success. In the eighteenth century there was more correlation, but, after Rousseau, it was correlation inspired by the sovereignty of the child rather than by the relations between school studies. Emile learned what was suitable for his nature at the time when his nature called for it, without regard to subject boundaries and the different kinds of knowledge that came to him were fused through his experience.

The same principle as developed by Pestalozzi (1746–1827) led Wilhelm Harnisch (1787–1864) to work out a fusion program for fields of instruction called by the Germans *Realien*. In his *Welt-kunde,* published in 1817, Harnisch brought together in one organization the following eight subjects: geography, mineralogy, physics, botany, zoology, anthropology, statistics, and history.

There were three circles in the program, and in each circle materials from all of the eight subjects were arranged in the order in which the pupil's nature might be assumed to call for them. The child must begin with his own little world and not with the world of his teacher. So the first circle is *Heimatkunde*. It embraces the school, the home, and the immediate community. The second circle is *Vaterlandskunde*. It embraces Germany. The third circle is *Erdkunde*. It embraces the world.

History as it appears in this combination is, in the first circle, local history, in the second circle, German history, and in the third circle, world history.

Heimatkunde made a lasting impression in Germany. Many varieties have been worked out since Harnisch wrote but always there has been *Heimatkunde,* and to Harnisch is awarded the honor of being called its father. His *Vaterlands-kunde* and *Erdkunde* were received less favorably and by later critics were regarded as achievements in confusion, rather than in fusion. They were in reality examples of what afterward came to be called *concentration,* with geography as the central subject. History was completely disorganized and reduced to disconnected fragments of information for the accommodation of geography.

Jean Joseph Jacotot (1770–1840) in a work on education published in 1822 proposed another kind of correlation. "All," he said, "is in all" (*tout est dans tout*). Therefore, learn one thing thoroughly and relate everything to that.

Jacotot selected Fénelon's *Télémaque* as the one thing to be learned thoroughly and made that the center of everything to be taught. Télémaque was, of course, Telemachus of the *Odyssey* searching for his father. "A Greek poem in French prose," Voltaire called it. But Fénelon used the familiar adventures as vehicles for conveying political and moral lessons to Frenchmen in the age of Louis XIV and thus supplied a wide range of materials for testing Jacotot's theory.

The *Odyssey* itself had already been used as a foundation in education. Johann Friedrich Herbart (1776–1841) had thus used it in tutoring three boys in a Swiss family. He remained a tutor for two years and in the course of this experience developed, at about the age of twenty-one, a complete theory of education. In the forty-four years that followed he amplified his theory. He supported it by psychology and philosophy. He undertook to elevate education to a science, but to the end the *Odyssey* remained his starting-point.

Herbart summed up the whole aim of education in the word "morality," and this aim, as he conceived it, required for its promotion a fullness of knowledge not to be attained through education according to the theories of Rousseau or Pestalozzi. Emile's kind of education, through experience, would always be difficult and could never fit any one to live in society, and education through experience in conventional society would only perpetuate existing evils. The best education must come through *instruction*. "Fill the minds of children," said Herbart, "and give them a many-sided interest." For this purpose Herbart would lay the whole known world in all ages under tribute. Beginning with the *Odyssey* he would have children follow from stage to stage the experience of the race. He does not explicitly formulate the culture epoch theory, but his program suggests that he had the idea.

There was one limitation. "Periods," says Herbart, "which no master has described, whose spirit no poet breathes, are of little value to education." As for the interest of children, that is something which teachers can control, and they should not hesitate to control it.

History holds a primary place in Herbart's theory. He outlines a separate course in history. He also suggests approaches to history through other subjects. He would have the teacher of geography, for example, note that the works of man on the earth are not so old as mountains, rivers, and oceans; that years ago the country looked different, and that people then did not do things just as they do them now. Passing from country to country in this way, the pupil would gather information which later could be welded together in the history course.

In dealing with history, Herbart shows that history without geography is unintelligible, and he also draws upon language and literature, but in his actual correlation, Herbart does not advance beyond earlier writers.[1]

Herbart exerted little influence on education during his lifetime, and when he died his theory was apparently buried with him, and rested in oblivion until Tuiskon Ziller (1817–1882) in 1865 published a treatise based upon Herbart's ideas. Ziller and other exponents of Herbart came to be known as the *Herbartians,* and through their works Herbart rose to become a major luminary in the educational firmament.

Herbart had suggested that the pupil should study all subjects and be able to grasp their unifying relations so as to have in his mind an articulated body of knowledge and opinions. Ziller took this hint and worked out a unified curriculum for the elementary school on the principle of *concentration,* which means the grouping of everything to be taught about one central subject. Ziller chose history as his central subject and

[1] See A. K. Ottelin, *Herbartiansk Historieundervisning,* Helsingfors, 1908.

in the grading of the materials consciously formulated the culture epoch theory. According to this theory, materials for the child should be drawn from the childhood of the race, materials for the boy should be drawn from the boyhood of the race, and so on, through youthhood to manhood. The theory was old. There are hints of it in antiquity. But Ziller appears to have been the first to apply it fully in the making of a school curriculum.

There were Herbartians who objected to history as a central subject. Some of them used general science instead. Some of them used geography. Some of them used the social life of the school. Some of them used current events. The literature is voluminous. In 1900 it was estimated that in Germany and Switzerland alone the printing presses had turned out more than two thousand books on the Herbartian movement.

The movement reached the United States and in the 90's assumed large proportions. Here it was usually called *correlation,* though strict Herbartians continued to call it *concentration.* Subject boundaries were attacked, often with great heat, and often the cry was raised, "Down with school subjects!" Again and again it was remarked that just about the time you begin to get children interested, some one comes along and smites them with a subject.

Leaders like Doctor Charles de Garmo, Doctor Charles McMurry, Doctor Frank McMurry, and Colonel Francis W. Parker were able to present Herbartian views in a manner that commanded serious and widespread attention. The McMurry brothers with their skill in classroom teaching and their writings on methods of teaching influenced very directly the shaping of school programs. Correlation was taken seriously by the Committee of Ten reporting on secondary education to the National Education Association in 1894, and still more seriously by the Committee of Fifteen reporting on elementary education to the same Association in 1895. Neither report, however, achieved full correlation in the Herbartian sense, and after 1900 a decline in general interest became apparent.

The five formal steps which were the chief contribution of the Herbartians to methods of teaching had by that time been found applicable with or without correlation, and the emphasis placed upon them tended to obscure the issue of correlation. By that time also the issue had been further obscured by the enthusiasm of converts to what was called *close correlation.*

Close correlation produced lessons of a type that often seemed absurd. A lesson on the egg, for example, might use arithmetic in weighing and measuring the egg, geography in exhibiting the egg as an article of commerce, nature study in contemplating the presence of a possible chick, literature through *Humpty-Dumpty,* and history through the egg story about Columbus. At the end there might be a composition by the pupil on "Eggs That I Have Eaten," and when the pupil that night told his parents about the egg lesson they laughed in derision. Soon the great American public laughed, and close correlation collapsed with some damage to more respectable correlation.

The use of one school study as the central core of the curriculum failed of general acceptance. History as the core seemed to spoil natural science. Natural science as the core seemed to spoil history. Whatever the core, other studies suffered a disorganization that seemed to rob them of salient values.

Within the last twenty years such general correlation has given way in the United States to a narrower correlation within certain groups of studies, so that we now have *general science, general mathematics,* and the *social studies.*

The Committee on Social Studies in Secondary Education in 1916 forgot the Herbartians and reverted to earlier ways of thinking. More recent reformers have revived dreams of the kind of fusion that Franciscus Balduinus dreamed in 1561, making *fusion* and *integration* words as potent in the 1920's as *concentration* and *correlation* were in the 90's. Many schools have dropped the word *history* and put in *social studies.* Programs with the latter label have been rated by Curriculum Bureaus as *progressive.* Separate courses in history have been rated as *antiquated.* Yet reports from the field indicate that in social studies programs each of the social studies is still taught separately, with some attention to correlation, but without real fusion. The nearest approach to fusion is perhaps found in a type of program which suggests a return to the principle of concentration with history as the binding core of the social studies. For bolder spirits bent upon a more comprehensive fusion or integration there might be hints in a book by Mark Hopkins first published in 1878 and entitled *An Outline Study of Man*.[2]

[2] The materials used for Chapters XI, XII, and XIII are in part either documented in earlier chapters or suggested in the body of the text. More specific references would, owing to the range and brevity of the treatment, have swamped the text in footnotes.

Chapter XII

FITTING THE PAST TO THE PRESENT

The principle that what to teach about the past should be determined by the present requires for its application some preliminary analysis of the present to be served. At the outset varying degrees of provincialism appear.

What history should be studied by boys and girls living in the United States in 1932? Not of course the history studied by boys and girls living in 1932 in England or France or Germany. That may be described as a mildly progressive view of history for schools.

What history should be studied by boys and girls living in the State of New York in 1932? Not of course the history studied by boys and girls living in 1932 in South Carolina or Illinois or California. That is more progressive.

What history should be studied by boys and girls living in New York City in 1932? Not of course the history studied by boys and girls living in 1932 in Albany or Rochester or Buffalo. That is radical.

119

What history should be studied by boys and girls in attendance in 1932 at Public School No. 14 in New York City? Not of course the history studied by their contemporaries in Public School No. 13 or in Public School No. 15. That is more radical.

What history should be studied by John who is thinking this morning that some day it might be interesting to be President of the United States? Not of course the history studied by Charles who wants to be another Babe Ruth or by James who wants to be a railroad conductor. What history should be studied by Adeline who is dreaming of an operatic career? Not of course the kind of history studied by Patricia who is cultivating the manners of a duchess, or by Susan, who has a way of inspiring boy poets to search the dictionary for words that rhyme with Susan. That is radical beyond the peradventure of a doubt.

For mild progressives it is sufficient to fit the past to the United States in 1932 by providing a United States history of the world and a United States history of the United States. For advances toward radicalism there will, in accord with the degree of advance, be need of a New York State history of the world and a New York State history of the United States, a New York City history of the world and a New York City history of the United States, and so on to a children's "inner urge" history of indefinable scope.

On the same principle and quite in harmony with some of our educational philosophy, history for schools may meet present needs in an American Legion history of the United States, a Knights of Columbus history of the United States, a Sons or Daughters of the American Revolution history of the United States, an American Federation of Labor history of the United States. Any social group with clear views of present needs is within its rights in calling upon history in schools to meet those needs.

Adjustment to a present educational horizon, whatever its span, has tended from the beginning to turn history into propaganda for predetermined ideals of life and conduct. It has led to much innocent distortion of facts and proportions and to some deliberate falsification. The world history that we read in German textbooks is not the world history that we read in French textbooks or in American textbooks. There are variations in the selection of facts and still greater variations in emphasis and interpretation. The France that we read about in French textbooks is different from the France that we read about in German textbooks. The United States that we read about in American textbooks is very different from the United States that we read about in European textbooks. Every country finds in its history as presented in the schools of other countries sources of irritation and at home assumes impeccability in teaching the history of other countries.

Adjustment to a present educational horizon besides making history provincial has made history as ephemeral as the present which it serves. Here in the United States, for example, it was pointed out early in the World War that the establishment of friendship between the United States and Great Britain would be the greatest thing in the world for civilization. There were obstacles, and a retired New York banker and others discovered that one of the obstacles was the treatment of the American Revolution in

American textbooks. We were therefore urged to teach a new kind of American Revolution, a Revolution that would make for friendship with Great Britain. In numberless speeches the unhappy differences between eighteenth-century Americans and eighteenth-century Englishmen happily disappeared. Even eighteenth-century Americans disappeared, and there remained only Englishmen living on opposite sides of the Atlantic, Englishmen with common interests, common traditions, and common aspirations. The root of the whole trouble was not in colonial grievances against Great Britain. It was in the German blood of George III, and against that bad blood Englishmen on both sides of the Atlantic were arrayed. This kind of American Revolution found its way into some new textbooks produced during the war and was reflected in some revisions of old textbooks.

Before the World War closed, however, Sons and Daughters of the American Revolution began to ask why their ancestors went to war if there were no serious differences with Great Britain. Knights of Columbus were not sure that they favored a new kind of American Revolution, just to be friendly with Great Britain. Mayor Thompson, of Chicago, and other one hundred per cent patriots, many of them in State legislatures, began to worry about the good name of the fathers of our Republic. A nation-wide attack was instituted against American textbooks "subsidized" by Great Britain.

Many times in the three hundred years since history became a separate school study have similar issues arisen to disturb the repose of theorists thrilling with the discovery that what to teach about the past should be determined by the present.

Just now a theory seems to be spreading in the United States that history should be democratized. It has even been intimated that a little knowledge of history is a possible handicap in drafting a history program for schools. Only a person without special knowledge of the subject, it is said, is qualified to determine the objectives of history and therefore the nature of the content. It is admitted, however, that the views of a single ignorant person may be somewhat subjective. To reach a scientific level there are appeals to other ignorant persons and when statistics show what five hundred or one thousand ignorant persons think about history one may be sure of having found the kind of history that is acceptable to an uninformed public, the kind of history that the man in the street really wants in the schools, and, therefore, a properly democratized kind of history.

There is one serious difficulty. Some millions of Americans organized in some thousands of "pressure groups" have formulated conflicting demands, and broad as history is it cannot quite be all things to all men. The general result is that history has become, to a degree new in the United States, a controversial subject. We have been rapidly moving in that direction since about 1918, and if we go on may produce a condition that will force history out of the public school curriculum and relegate it to the domain to which religion has already been relegated.

CHAPTER XIII

USING THE PAST TO EXPLAIN THE PRESENT

The idea of using the past to explain the present, while often implicit in earlier discussions of history as a school subject, rarely received explicit emphasis until the latter part of the nineteenth century. History for schools was called upon to furnish recreation and entertainment, to illuminate the classics, to set up examples of conduct, good and bad, to supply vicarious experience, to offer practice in reading the human heart, to serve as a mirror in which the pupil might see himself, to support religion, to inculcate patriotism, and, in general, to build up predetermined ideals and stimulate predetermined kinds of behavior. In all these ways what passed for history could minister to immediate needs without explaining either the past or the present.

Early practice tended to focus upon ancient history. This was partly because the materials were more available and in a better literary form and partly because school learning consisted chiefly in learning to read Latin (after awhile Greek was added), and partly because ancient history seemed to be richer in the desired kind of examples than even the history of the pupil's own country. There were from the first advocates of the history of the fatherland, and eventually their cause was won, but Rollin spoke for French practice in the eighteenth century when, admitting that the history of France was desirable, he argued that ancient history was more useful and that there was not time in school for both. In the nineteenth century, French programs, until 1865, consistently ignored contemporary history and after that wavered. In Germany, at the opening of the nineteenth century, a German could still ask, "Shall we go on knowing more about the history of Greece and of Rome than of the history of our own country?" and as late as 1860 official German programs commonly ended with the Middle Ages.

In the United States as late as 1895, the Committee of Fifteen proposed that the study of American history in the elementary school should end with the adoption of the Constitution. In

England, orthodox teachers even in the twentieth century have held that English history should end with the accession of Victoria.

Such programs were effective in setting up desired kinds of examples and ideals, and were further supported by a theory that contemporary history bristled with too many controversies to be suitable for school instruction.

There were, however, precedents for a different view. Christian Weise in the seventeenth century set out to give Saxon boys an understanding of Saxony in their own times. Asking frankly why boys living in Saxony in 1676 should study ancient history, he prescribed contemporary history and current events. Joseph Priestley deliberately used history in the eighteenth century for the purpose of explaining to English boys their own times and carried the idea farther than most history programs carry it now. Throughout the eighteenth century, current events figured among requirements laid down in school regulations and were so related to historical instruction as to suggest an interest in understanding the present.

During the Napoleonic wars history began to

turn to patriotism as its dominating objective and after 1815 national history rose rapidly to a dominating position in history programs for schools. It was, however, rarely national history brought down to date and therefore rarely reached an explanation of the present. Germans found in the Middle Ages the Germanism most desired in promoting German patriotism. Frenchmen and Englishmen stopped short of recent history to avoid clashes of controversy in the schools. Our Committee of Fifteen proposed stopping at 1789 because our history after that date had not yet become sufficiently "classic" for use in elementary schools. It was not until the nineties that the use of the past in explaining the present began to find general acceptance as a determining factor in shaping history for schools. Emphasis then shifted to contemporary history and still remains there.

The use of the past in explaining the present obviously implies an understanding of the past. If the past is not understood, the past can obviously contribute little toward an understanding of the present. This condition was recognized in the nineties and led to the conclusion (reached by Karl Müller in 1835) that history in school must, so far as it goes, be in harmony with historical scholarship. But historical scholarship was scientific. Its purpose, in Ranke's classic phrase, was merely to portray the past "as it actually was."[1] It was history for history's sake and, as such, subject to rigid scrutiny in planning history for immediate educational ends. That scrutiny has persisted and, guided always by the old principle that what to teach about the past should be determined by present needs, has so limited the selection of facts as sometimes to suggest that the past can be used in explaining the present without taking the trouble to make the past itself intelligible.

Continental European programs in history did rather early take over from scientific history the ideas of development and continuity. Karl Müller had those ideas and applied them and by 1890

[1] In the preface to his *Geschichten der römanischen und germanischen Völker*, 1824, Ranke writes that his purpose is not to essay the lofty task of judging the past nor of furnishing instruction for the present. *Er will bloss zeigen wie es eigentlich gewesen.* Ranke was then a young teacher of history in a German secondary school.

they had passed into general practice on the Continent. They were expressed in *courses* in history. England and the United States favored *subjects* in history. In the United States, for example, we have had in our secondary schools such *subjects* as ancient history, European history, French history, English history, American history, and Latin-American history. Continental Europeans in their secondary schools have had history, periodized, it is true, as ancient, medieval, modern, and contemporary, but as parts of a continuous *course* and not as separate *subjects*. The *course* idea was strongly recommended by the Madison Conference of 1892 but was rejected by the Committee of Ten and American thinking about history for schools is still usually in terms of subjects.

Continental European countries have not gone all the way to world history. The Germans have made Germany the center of their course and the French have made France the center. But either country, for obvious reasons, can be made the center of a course in world history in a sense not possible with the United States as a center, and both German and French programs have achieved complete continuity in tracing in a large way the development of humanity.

In the United States the weight of professional educational opinion has been against the ideas of development and continuity in history programs. The Committee on the Social Studies in 1916 expressly attacked the idea of continuity as "antiquated" and substituted for it ideas that were old in the eighteenth century. The bulk of our educational theorizing about history still proceeds as if determined to keep abreast with eighteenth-century theorizing. Most of our textbook writers during the past thirty-five years have taken a more advanced position, and many of them, within the limits imposed by our *subjects* in history, have traced with conspicuous success that ceaseless process of becoming which historians call development. For this they have often been accused of imposing upon schools history for history's sake. The charge does them too much honor. Textbooks are at best compromises with prevailing educational theories and are professedly written with one eye on the present. What educational critics really mean when they class text-books as history for history's sake is that history for schools should be written with *both* eyes on the present, a feat, it must be admitted, not yet achieved even by critics who have themselves set out to accomplish it.

Using the past to explain the present had by 1914 risen to a foremost place among objectives set up for history in schools. The World War magnified patriotism with consequences after 1918 similar to those in evidence after 1815, but with more dissenting voices. Patriotic history appealed especially to new countries created by the war. The war itself furnished abundant materials. In defeated countries the problem of adjustment to changed conditions was more difficult. The war materials, if brought down to date, were not inspiring and the old traditions did not fit. In Russia the old traditions were simply eliminated. History practically disappeared and current problems were treated in a manner to support the new régime. Among the victors the history of the war was taught in schools with patriotic fervor and bias and some new pride in old traditions. The greatest change was in Italy where history was made over to fit the ideals of fascism. The smallest change was in France. There the old history, having stood the test of war, was still regarded, in the main, as satisfactory.

In the United States, since about 1912, history has been turning more and more to an explanation of vital current problems. In that direction we have probably gone farther than any other people. In the social studies movement, which may be regarded as an extreme expression of this tendency, we have gone so far that current problems are now to the social studies what examples of conduct were to history in the eighteenth century. History, that is, now revolves around current problems in about the way that history in the eighteenth century revolved around examples of conduct. The principle in both cases is to take out of the past only what is directly useful in the present.

The approach to the past through current problems has the merit of being relatively easy, especially when it proceeds by topics. Having decided what topics are important—railroads, automobiles, airplanes, transportation in general, prohibition, the tariff, depression—the program maker need only turn to standard works of reference to find materials already put together in the form of historical sketches. If he wants more details he finds them already conveniently grouped in special treatises. Even when special treatises run to hundreds of pages, topics presented separately after the manner of an encyclopedia are much more easily managed than the total mass movement which the general historian must analyze and organize.

The topical plan while announced in the United States as new in its application to history in school, has also been thought of in other countries. It was the plan of Comenius in 1632. It was the plan of Haupt in 1841. Even in the United States the plan is not altogether new. It was to some extent tested here in the eighties, following the publication of John J. Lalor's *Cyclopedia of Political Science, Political Economy, and of the Political History of the United States,* three volumes, Chicago, 1881–1884, a work that is still useful for its topics.

Within the topics selected, social studies programs often impress very skillfully the idea of development. Whether this piecemeal method of explaining the present can ever be adequate is another question. Every course of human development is so bound up with every other course of human development that a piecemeal treatment may fail to explain even the pieces at which it aims. Older schemes, like those of Comenius and Haupt, sought to overcome this difficulty by bringing all the pieces together for a general survey at the end of the course. But Weise in 1676 and Müller in 1835 maintained that the pieces must be kept together throughout the course.

To seek the easiest and the shortest road to the use of the past in explaining the present is natural and proper. But any road that really reaches the desired end must make the past which it traverses intelligible and must, therefore, lead to what mattered *then* on the way to what matters *now*.

INDEX

Adjusting to interests of pupils, 8, 9, 29

Ahasuerus, use of history by, 9

Ancient history, 29, 103, 126 ff.

Ancient, medieval and modern history classification, 34 (*See* also Divisions of history)

Approach through story of inventions, 17, 18

Balduinus, Franciscus, 107 ff.

Basedow, Johann Bernhard, 73–82

Biographical approach to history, 56, 57

Campe, Johann Heinrich, 84 ff.

Cellarius, Christoph (Keller), 34

Central position of history, 22, 112, 114, 116

Changing world, education for, 3, 4, 21

Chart of biography, 68 (*See* also Devices of instruction)

Chart of history, 67 (*See* also Devices of instruction)

Charts, 30 (*See* also Devices of instruction)

Chronological charts, 44 (*See* also Devices of instruction)

Civics, training for citizenship, 12, 21, 34, 62, 63, 68, 71, 72, 77, 80, 81, 89, 90, 93, 94 (*See* also Objectives and History, uses of)

Class size, 70

Comenius, 31, 32, 33, 135, 136

Committee of Fifteen, 115, 127, 129

Committee of Ten, 58, 115, 131

Committee on the Social Studies, 58, 132

Community concerns as center, 41, 85 ff. (*See* also Curriculum, guiding principles)

Compayre, Gabriel, 31

Comprehensive history, 63–67, 101–102, 107 (*See* also History, kinds of)

Compulsory education, 89

Concentration, 110, 114, 117 (*See* also Curriculum, guiding principles)

Concentric circles, 103 (*See* also Curriculum, guiding principles)

Contemporary history, 42, 93, 128 ff.

Continuity of development of society, 25, 34, 103, 132 (*See* Curriculum, guiding principles)

Core subjects, 22, 54–56 (*See* also Curriculum, guiding principles)

Correlation with various subjects, 82, 107, 108, 109, 112, 114, 116–118 (*See* also Curriculum, guiding principles)

Cosmopolitanism, history for, 81

Courses vs. subjects, 131 ff.

Critical treatment of history in schools, 19, 26, 52, 54, 70, 91, 103, 104

Cultivating judgment, 20, 23, 93 (*See* also Objectives)

Culture epoch theory, 112, 114 (*See* Curriculum, guiding principles)

Current events, 9, 42, 64 ff., 114, 128

Current problems approach, 134

Curricula, examples, 31–32, 63–67, 75–76, 103–105

Curriculum, guiding principles in construction of, serving needs of present, 1–2, 24, 39, 75–76, 93, 98, 103, 114, 130–35; community concerns as center, 41, 85–86; modern problems as centre, 39, 134; proceeding from present to past, 39, 42, 75–76, 114, 130–35; newspapers, 42; adjusting to interests of pupils, 8, 9, 29, 50, 58, 111, 112, 114; preparation for college, 29; culture epoch theory, 112, 114; biographical approach, 56; approach through story of inventions, 17, 18; from the particular to the general and from the general to the whole, 101; concentric circles, 103; cycles, 103; circles, 109; continuity of development of society, 25, 34, 103, 132; *Four Monarchies,* 25; periods of history, 34; correlation with various subjects, 82, 102, 107, 108, 109, 112, 114, 116, 117, 118; *close correlation,* 116; fusion, 107, 109, 117, 118; *tout est dans tout,* 110; integration, 117 ff.; core subjects, 22, 54–56; propaganda for pressure groups, 121, 122; propaganda for nationalism, 121–22, 125, 133; courses vs. subjects, 131; developmental principle, 22, 132 ff.

Curtius, Quintus, 34

Cycles, 103 (*See* also Curriculum, guiding principles)

Daily review, 38 (*See* also Devices of instruction)

Dates, use in teaching history, 36–37, 40, 103; method of teaching, 40–41

De Garmo, Dr. Charles, 115

Dessau, 80 ff., 84

Developmental principle, 22, 132 ff.

Devices of instruction, pictures, 1, 30, 81; map and globes, 37; globes, 40, 153; motion pictures, 4; charts, 30; chart of biography, 68; chart of history, 67; chronological charts, 44; written exercises, 71; writing of history by pupils, 83; note-books, 83; work-books, 83; map-making by pupils, 53; questioning, 45; questions by pupils, 38, 71; "tell-me" questions, 44–45; true-false questions, 83; reversing questions, 45; recitation, 44; discussion, 46; spell-down, 83; problem setting, 45, 53, 71, 82, 83; informal lecture, 71; relating material to life, 46; reading aloud, 42; diversifying material, 46–47, 83; sources, 2, 63, 70, 91, 103, 104; sagas, 84; drama, 81; games, 89; festivals, 81; daily review, 38; drill, 38, 83; textbooks, 13, 14, 16, 17, 18, 23–29, 32, 78 ff., 81 ff., 92 ff., 104 ff., 121 ff., 132; newspaper, 42 (*See* also Methods of instruction)

Dewey, John, 59

Didactic history for religion, 13 (*See* also History, uses of)

Diestelmann, R., 86

Dietrich of Niem, 16

Discussion, 46 (*See* also Devices of instruction)

Drama, 81 (*See* also Devices of instruction)

Drills, daily, 38, 83 (*See* also Devices of instruction)

Education as life, 50, 58, 85, 117, 118, 119
Elementary education, 6, 31, 32, 33, 36–45, 73, 76, 80, 105, 111, 112, 113, 116, 119
Ellis, 18
Emile, 50–60, 74, 76, 96
English history, 128 (*See* also History, kinds of)
Erasmus, 20
Erdkunde, 109
Euclid, 24
Eutropius, 13, 34

Fénelon, 110
Festivals, 81 (*See* also Devices of instruction)
Flexner, Dr. Abraham, 1
Florus, 13
Four Monarchies, 24 ff., 28, 29, 35, 41
Foxley, 52
France, history since World War, 134
Frederick the Great, 19, 87 ff.
French history, 29 (*See* History, kinds of)
Frontier thinking, 2, 3, 4, 5
Fusion, 107 ff., 109, 110, 117, 118

Gallandt, Julius, 86
Games, 57, 89 (*See* Devices of instruction)
Gaspari, 96
Genealogy, 81
Geographical knowledge essential to history, 23, 38, 53, 103, 112
Geography, 38, 39, 53, 64; as central subject, 110, 114; correlation with history, 29, 82
Grade placement, 28, 31, 51, 100
Greek history, 29, 30, 127 (*See* also History, kinds of)
Gregory of Tours, 16

Harnisch, Wilhelm, 108 ff.
Haupt, 135, 136
Hecatæus, 106
Heimatkunde, 109
Heraldry, 81
Herbart, Johann Friedrich, 111 ff.
Herbartians, 113 ff.
Herodotus, 10, 11, 12, 55, 63, 106
Historia Anglorum, 29
History, divisions and kinds of, Four Monarchies, 24 ff., 28, 29; Ancient, Medieval, Modern, 34; Universal history, 26; Ancient history, 29, 103, 126; comprehensive history, 63–67, 101–02, 107; English history, 128; French history, 29; Greek history, 29, 30, 127; *Kulturgeschichte,* 94; military history, 23; political history, 67, 93; Roman history, 29, 30, 127
History, uses of, 21, 97, 126; for diversion, 9, 11, 22, 34, 63, 126; functioning in present, 10, 16, 23; as preparation for future, 12, 18; "philosophy teaching by examples," 12–13, 19, 21, 34, 77, 80; didactic history for religion, 13; morals, 12; ideals of life, 12; patriotism, 12, 128; to acquaint people with their rights, 21; to give meaning to all learning, 99; to avoid wasted effort, 99; for social control, 21; "mistress of prudence and civil knowledge," 34; understanding of "human heart" or motives, 55–58; for training of leaders in affairs, 34; training of prince, 77, 89–90; training of subjects, 80; training of statesmen and citizens, 62, 63; as branch of litera-

Index

ture, 10, 11, 12, 106; as central subject, 22, 112 ff.; defects of, according to Rousseau, 54–56; superior value of ancient history, 56, 57; for orientation and to view contemporary events in perspective, 20, 30, 80, 90, 91 (*See* also Objectives)

Hopkins, Mark, 118

Hume, David, 49, 50

Ideals of life, 12, 18, 22, 91 (*See* also Objectives)

Ilfeld am Harz, 28

Informal lecture, 71 (*See* also Devices of instruction)

Integration, 102, 106 ff., 117 (*See* also Curriculum, guiding principles)

Interest of pupils controlled by teacher, 112

International outlook, 81

Italy, history since World War, 134

Jacotot, Jean Joseph, 110

Joshua, 8, 9, 10

Justinius, 34

Keatinge, 33

Keferstein, H., 20

Kipling, R., 47

Kulturgeschichte, 94

Lalor, John J., 135

Lecture, 68–71 (*See* also Methods of instruction)

Libraries, for pupils, 29

Livy, 13, 55

Locke, John, 34

Luther, 19, 20

Madison Conference, 131

Map-making by pupils, 53 (*See* also Devices of instruction)

Maps and Globes, 37, 38, 40

(*See* also Devices of instruction)

McMurry, Dr. Charles, 115

McMurry, Dr. Frank, 115

Methodenbuch, 77

Methods of instruction, 75; oral, 30; oral expression, 43; lecture, 68–71; informal lecture, 71; recitation, 44; socialized recitation, 38; discussion, 46; problem setting, 45, 53, 71, 82, 83; project, 8, 51; avoidance of task element, 33 (*See* also Devices of instruction)

Military history, 23

Mirror idea in history, 19, 20, 21, 30, 47, 77

Modern problems as center of curriculum, 39, 134 (*See* also Curriculum, guiding principles)

Morals, 12, 18, 22, 30, 91, 92, 111 (*See* also Objectives)

More, Sir Thomas, 20

Motion pictures, 4 (*See* also Devices of instruction)

Motivation, use of "inner urge," 9

Müller, Karl August, 95, 130, 136

Mythology, 81, 86

National history, 16, 18, 121–22, 128

Neander, Michael, 28

Needs of the present as a basis for curriculum construction, 1–2, 98

Nepos, Cornelius, 13

Newspapers, 42 (*See* also Devices of instruction)

Note-books, 83 (*See* also Devices of instruction)

Objectives
Use of history for diversion,

Index

9, 22; Patriotism, 12, 16, 18, 29, 72, 91; Ideals of life, 12, 18, 22, 91; Morals, 12, 18, 22, 30, 91, 92; religion, 13, 18, 22; for orientation and to view contemporary events in perspective, 20, 30, 80, 90, 91; cultivating judgment, 20, 23, 93; international outlook, 81; tolerance, 91 (*See* also Civics, and History, uses of)
Oral expression, 42, 43 (*See* also Methods of instruction)
Oratorians, 29, 30
Orosius, 15
Ottelin, A. K., 113
Oxford, 20

Parker, Colonel Francis W., 115
Patriotism, 12, 16, 17, 18, 29, 67, 72, 81, 91, 126, 129, 133 (*See* also Objectives)
Periods of history, 34 (*See* also Curriculum, guiding principles)
Pestalozzi, 108, 111
"Philosophy teaching by examples," 12-13, 19, 21, 34, 77, 86 (*See* also History, uses of)
Pictures, 1, 30, 81 (*See* also Devices of instruction)
Pinloche, 86
Plutarch, 57
Political history, 67, 93, 94 (*See* also History, kinds of)
Political Science (*See* Civics)
Polybius, 55
Pressure groups, 121, 123 ff., 125
Priestley, Joseph, 61–72, 96, 103
Problem setting, 45, 53, 71, 82, 83 (*See* also Devices of instruction)
Progressive education, 3–4; based on belief that history repeats itself, 13
Project method, 8, 51

Propaganda, for nationalism, 121–22, 125, 133; for pressure groups, 121–22 (*See* also Curriculum, guiding principles)

Questioning, 38, 45, 71 (*See* also Devices of instruction)

Ranke, 130
Reading aloud, 42 (*See* also Devices of instruction)
Recitation, 44 (*See* also Devices of instruction)
Reformation, 23 ff.
Reim, Carl, 28
Relationship of history to other subjects, 22 (*See* also Curriculum, guiding principles)
Religion, 12, 18, 22 (*See* also Objectives)
Richelieu, 30
Robinson, J. H., 10, 11
Rollin, 127
Roman history, 29, 30, 127 (*See* also History, kinds of)
Rosenburg, Hermann, 15
Rousseau, 3, 48–60, 92, 108, 111
Russia, history in, since World War, 133

Sagas, 84 (*See* also Devices of instruction)
Sallust, 55
Salzmann, C. G., 85 ff., 101
Secondary education, 19, 28, 31, 53 ff., 62–72, 73, 80–86
Severus, Sulpicius, 13
Sex hygiene, 76
Sleidanus, Johannes, 23, 24, 25, 26, 28, 29, 34, 35
Social history, 17, 32, 63–67, 76, 94 (*See* also History, kinds of)
Social Studies, 117 ff., 134

Socialized recitation, 38 (*See* also Methods of instruction)
Sociology (*See* Social studies)
Sources, 2, 63, 70, 91, 103, 104 (*See* also Devices of instruction)
Suetonius, 57

Tacitus, 55
Task element, avoidance of, 33 (*See* also Methods of instruction)
Teacher of history, character and training, 86, 100, 103, 104, 105
Textbooks, 13, 14, 16, 17, 18, 23–29, 32, 78 ff., 81 ff., 92 ff., 104 ff., 121 ff., 132 (*See* also Devices of instruction)
Thorpe, T. E., 72
Thucydides, 12, 55
Tolerance, 91 (*See* also Objectives)
Topical organization of material, 32, 134
Trapp, Christian Ernst, 82 ff.
Trier, 17
True-false tests, 82, 83
Truth in history, 55, 82–83, 91, 92, 104 (*See* also Critical treatment)

Unit organization of material, 32; weakness of, 44, 101
United States Bureau of Education, 58
Universal history, 26 (*See* also History, divisions of)

Varro, 19
Vaterlandskunde, 109 ff.
Viskavatov, Pavel, 19
Visual aids, 30, 44, 52, 62, 68, 69, 81
Vives, Juan Luis, 3, 20–23
Volkschule, 6, 105
Voltaire, 63

War in history, 23 (*See* also Military history)
Watson, Foster, 23
Weise, Christian, 36–38, 40–47, 96, 108, 128, 136
Wimpheling, Jacob, 16–19
Workbooks, 83

Ziller, Tuiskon, 113 ff.

The exact titles of the various reports of this Commission cannot yet be definitely announced. The following is a list of the subject matter of the reports and the tentative titles as nearly as these can be determined at the time of this announcement:

1. A Charter for the Social Sciences in the Schools, by Charles A. Beard, formerly Professor of Politics, Columbia University.
2. An Introduction to the History of the Social Sciences in Schools, by Henry Johnson, Professor of History, Teachers College, Columbia University.
3. Citizens' Organizations and the Civic Training of Youth, by Bessie Louise Pierce, Associate Professor of American History, University of Chicago.
4. The Pupil's Approach to the Understanding of Society, by Truman L. Kelley, Professor of Education, Harvard University, and A. C. Krey, Professor of History, University of Minnesota.
5. Services of Geography to the Social Sciences, by Isaiah Bowman, Director, American Geographic Society of New York, with special studies by Rose Clark, Nebraska Wesleyan University; Edith Parker, University of Chicago; and R. D. Calkins, Central State Teachers College, Michigan.
6. Education in an Industrial Age, by George S. Counts, Professor of Education, Teachers College, Columbia University, and Charles A. Beard.
7. Materials and Instruction in the Social Science Programs, by Rolla M. Tryon, Professor of the Teaching of History, University of Chicago.
8. Methods of Instruction in the Social Sciences, by Ernest Horn, Professor of Education, University of Iowa.

9. Civic Training in the United States, by Charles E. Merriam, Professor of Political Science, University of Chicago.

10. School Administration and Social Science Teaching, by Jesse H. Newlon, Director, Lincoln School, Teachers College, Columbia University.

11. The Selection and Training of the Teacher, by William C. Bagley, Professor of Education, Teachers College, Columbia University; Guy Stanton Ford, Professor of History and Dean of the Graduate School, University of Minnesota; and others.

12. Freedom of Teaching in the Schools, by Howard K. Beale, formerly Professor of History at Bowdoin College.

13. Social Ideas of American Educators, by Merle Curti, Professor of History at Smith College.

14. Experimentation with Social Science Reading Materials, by C. H. Judd, Head of the Department of Education and Dean of the School of Education, University of Chicago.

15. Conclusions and Recommendations of the Commission.

Other volumes or reports have been projected, dealing with the history of the social ideas of American educational leaders and with the problem of freedom of teaching or the growth of tolerance in the teaching of these subjects.

It is also planned to publish a number of miscellaneous studies, many of them of an exploratory character, which have been made for the committee in one connection or another.

To be published by Charles Scribner's Sons.

COMMISSION ON DIRECTION

FRANK W. BALLOU, Superintendent of Schools, Washington, D. C.

CHARLES A. BEARD, formerly Professor of Politics, Columbia University; author of many books in the fields of history and politics.

ISAIAH BOWMAN, Director, American Geographic Society of New York; President of the International Geographical Union.

ADA COMSTOCK, President of Radcliffe College.

GEORGE S. COUNTS, Professor of Education, Teachers College, Columbia University.

AVERY O. CRAVEN, Professor of History, University of Chicago.

EDMUND E. DAY, formerly Dean of School of Business Administration, University of Michigan; now Director of Social Sciences, Rockefeller Foundation.

GUY STANTON FORD, Professor of History, Dean of the Graduate School, University of Minnesota.

CARLETON J. H. HAYES, Professor of History, Columbia University.

ERNEST HORN, Professor of Education, University of Iowa.

HENRY JOHNSON, Professor of History, Teachers College, Columbia University.

A. C. KREY, Professor of History, University of Minnesota.

LEON C. MARSHALL, Institute for the Study of Law, Johns Hopkins University.

CHARLES E. MERRIAM, Professor of Political Science, University of Chicago.

JESSE H. NEWLON, Professor of Education, Teachers College, Columbia University; Director of Lincoln Experimental School.

JESSE F. STEINER, Professor of Sociology, University of Washington.